The Kabbalah of Forgiveness

The Kabbalah of Forgiveness

The Thirteen Levels of Mercy
In Rabbi Moshe Cordovero's
Date Palm of Devorah (Tomer Devorah)

Henry Abramson

2018
Revised Edition

Cover design by Danit Mills

License Notes

This book is licensed for your personal enjoyment and information only. This book should not be re-sold to others. Educational institutions may reproduce, copy and distribute this book for non-commercial purposes without charge, provided appropriate citation of the source, in accordance with the Talmudic *dictum* of Rabbi Elazar in the name of Rabbi Hanina (*Megilah* 15a): "anyone who cites a teaching in the name of its author brings redemption to the world." This permission is intended for classroom use only. Small portions of the text may be posted on the Internet for review or study purposes.

Version 2.1
תשע"ח
2018

ISBN: 978-1500635718

First Published 2014

For my parents

Jack Abramson ע״ה and יבלח״ט Ethel Abramson of
Iroquois Falls, Ontario

who have forgiven so much

Other Works by Henry Abramson

Jewish History

A Prayer for the Government
Ukrainians and Jews in Revolutionary Times, 1917-1920

The Art of Hatred
Images of Intolerance in Florida Culture

Torah from the Years of Wrath 1939-1943
The Historical Context of the Aish Kodesh

Jewish Thought

Reading the Talmud
Developing Independence in Gemara Learning

The Sea of Talmud
A Brief and Personal Introduction

Maimonides on Teshuvah
The Ways of Repentance

Table of Contents

Approbation by Rabbi Ya'akov Trump

2 Preface
8 The Life and Work of Rabbi Moshe Cordovero
19 Introduction

The Kabbalah of Forgiveness

33 The First Level: The King who Endures Insult
45 The Second Level: Let it Go for Now
59 The Third Level: Take Care of It Personally
73 The Fourth Level: Remember the Family
91 The Fifth Level: Release the Anger
105 The Sixth Level: Who Makes Your Lunch?
121 The Seventh Level: A Knot is Stronger
139 The Eighth Level: Maintain a Core of Love
157 The Ninth Level: Bury the Past
175 The Tenth Level: Do the Right Thing Anyway
185 The Eleventh Level: Do More for Those Who Do More
195 The Twelfth Level: Remember Where They Came From
205 The Thirteenth Level: The Moment of Innocence
215 Conclusion

221 A Note on the Text
225 Select Bibliography

כל המעביר על מידותיו מעבירין לו על כל פשעיו

All who overcome their natural tendencies, will find that their own inadequacies are overlooked in divine judgment

Talmud Bavli, Rosh Hashana 17a

How does one find the key to growth in an increasingly complex world? The environment around us changes at an ever-increasing pace yet the maps to guide us through the new terrain always seem to be one step behind. This is not owing to a lack of attempted guidance. One is constantly assailed ideas, quotes and perspectives on social media, the subway walls and inspirational Memes. What is difficult to know is which of the values in tension really matters more in which situation. Is that inspirational quote an axiomatic truth or is it a nice idea sometimes applicable?

In Judaism, when we try to find answers we prefer to dig deeper than to spread the net broader. This book is a seminal work in that regard. R. Moshe Cordovero, in his work Tomer Devorah, describes the Kabbalistic underpinnings of divine judgement and then renders those deep metaphysical ideas into practical steps of self-improvement. This is essentially a practical guide how to be more Godly and how that impacts our relationship with God and others. One walks away from the book with both a more sincere appreciation of the complexity of the spiritual kingdom and also simple and practical behaviors which can be applied in day to day life.

Dr. Abramson's important translation is a significant step in disseminating these ideas to the wider public. Dr. Abramson not only translates the ideas into accessible English but also gives context to each of the thirteen ideas and illustrates these concepts with relevant and contemporary applications of the age-old Jewish wisdom. His translation and elucidation are a great service to the world.

Anyone who takes the time to truly read and learn this work will come out the other end as a significantly changed person.

May it be Hashem's will that we all grow together through the holy words of His Torah.

יעקב צבי שלאמן

Rabbi Ya'akov Zvi Trump

Associate Rabbi, Young Israel of Lawrence-Cedarhurst

Preface to the First Edition

Rabbi Moshe Cordovero's *Date Palm of Devorah* is a classic work of Jewish spirituality. Unparalleled for its unusual combination of esoteric Kabbalah, practical ethics, and profound insight into the potential for human greatness, it has been printed over seventy times and translated into many languages since it first appeared in 1588. A slim work of only 35 pages of Rabbinic Hebrew, it has had a signal impact on disparate areas of Jewish thought, including the study of Kabbalah, the development of Hasidism, and the Lithuanian *musar* movement. "Small in size but rich in quality," commented Rabbi Yom Tov Yedid of Jerusalem a century ago, giving expression to a thought that is shared by all who study *Date Palm of Devorah*.

I first encountered *Date Palm of Devorah* with the publication of Moshe Miller's translation in 1993. I had just turned thirty, and as I leafed through pages in a North Miami Beach bookstore I felt the thrilling invitation of the intellectually taboo, as my Lithuanian Orthodox background forbids the study of Kabbalah for students under forty (Rabbi Cordovero, incidentally, disagreed with this ban, arguing that Kabbalah should be taught to qualified students as young as twenty). *Date Palm of Devorah*, although suffused with Kabbalah, is generally considered to be exempt from that rule, and thus I read it cautiously, tentatively, and even furtively, foolishly concerned for the opinions of others.

It has been over twenty years since that day, and even now I am overwhelmed by the glorious first chapter, presented here in a new translation and with supporting commentary. I have taken the liberty of retitling this chapter as *The Kabbalah of Forgiveness*, since it deals with the immeasurable capacity for Divine mercy, and describes how we may draw from that infinite source to heal our fractured human relationships. In many ways the first chapter stands apart from the nine subsequent chapters in *Date Palm of Devorah*. It is considerably larger, taking up almost a third of the work as a whole, and it is far more accessible than the following chapters, which require much more Kabbalistic training to apprehend correctly. Students may benefit significantly by reading this first chapter alone, and I follow the example of many scholars who have excerpted this chapter as a stand-alone work.

The purpose of *The Kabbalah of Forgiveness* is to offer new readers an introduction to this life-changing work of Jewish thought. It is intended for those unfamiliar with the principles of Cordoveran Kabbalah and the classical Jewish ethics known as *musar*, although I hope that more advanced students may find *The Kabbalah of Forgiveness* useful as well. The measure of my success will be determined by the degree to which readers of *The Kabbalah of Forgiveness* will find inspiration to deepen their identification with the values of Judaism, improve their relationship with God, with others around them, and themselves.

Several English translations of *Date Palm of Devorah* have appeared, including the scholarly treatment of Louis Jacobs (1960) and the previously mentioned version by Moshe Miller. My translation will add little to these strong works. The value of my small contribution is in the updated introduction, which incorporates more recent scholarship, and the suggestions in the commentary for practical applications of *Date Palm of Devorah*. In this respect I take inspiration from the concept of Rebbetzin S. Feldbrand, whose 2007 work *Middos: Inspirations, Stories and Practical Advice Based on Tomer Devorah*, as well as

Rabbi Landau's *13 Midot: Tomer Devorah Perek Rishon* and Rabbi Shmuel Meir Riachi's *The Elucidated Tomer Devorah*, take related approaches.

Rabbis of great stature such as Rabbi Israel Salanter, the 19th century founder of the modern *musar* movement, and the 16th century Kabbalist Rabbi Levi Horowitz (the *Shelah ha-kodesh*) have advocated regular study of *Date Palm of Devorah* and testified that the book has great mystical power. The 19th century Hasidic master, Rabbi Hayim Halberstam of Sanz (author of *Divrei Hayim*) even asserted that the study of *Date Palm of Devorah* has the power to rescue a person from "that well-known disease," a euphemism for cancer. Pronouncements of this nature are beyond the scope of this humble translation and commentary, but I can state with confidence that *Date Palm of Devorah* has had a huge impact on my own life, giving me the spiritual and emotional resources to deal with challenging situations and difficult people.

One final note of caution: although I have steeped myself in Hebrew and Aramaic commentaries on *Date Palm of Devorah*, I am hardly a Kabbalist. I have had the privilege of learning under teachers well versed in Jewish mysticism, but in general our studies have always been in the realm of the revealed Torah of Talmud rather than the hidden Torah of Kabbalah. Rabbi Cordovero was somewhat unique among Kabbalists. He noted that unqualified teachers of Kabbalah are plenty, "arrogant in their knowledge… their voices crash like the waves of the sea, yet they possess not even a drop of wisdom," but he nevertheless advocated that students study this esoteric wisdom on their own, "even if they do not understand" (*Or Ne'erav*, 3). I write this small book in this spirit, as one who does not fully understand, and even as one who does not possess a drop of wisdom. Composing *The Kabbalah of Forgiveness* has been an act of personal piety, and I share my meditations in the sincere hope that other readers will also find benefit in humble introductory presentation to the thought of Rabbi Moshe Cordovero.

Has this study made me a more forgiving person? Absolutely, but it would be more correct to say that *Date Palm of Devorah* has made my many failures to forgive all the more obvious. Forgiveness, particularly regarding people with whom one interacts regularly, is not a switch that can be placed in the "on" position and left alone. Feelings of resentment, irritation and betrayal are incredibly hard to overcome, their periodic demands for attention retarding spiritual growth like noxious weeds that constantly invade even the most well-manicured garden of the mind. I am filled with regret for the many occasions that anger dominated my thinking like a dense and sulfuric fog, sometimes propelling me to act or speak inappropriately, but the contemplation of the Thirteen Levels of Mercy as described in *Date Palm of Devorah* always propelled me through negative emotions to a healthier state of thinking.

This book, a commentary on *Date Palm of Devorah*, consequently took quite a bit longer to write than originally intended. When I first began work on *The Kabbalah of Forgiveness* in the fall of 2012, I projected completion within six months. A year later, with even the first chapter still unfinished, I discovered an unusual phenomenon: try as I might, I simply could not bear working on the manuscript if I harbored feelings of resentment for any another person. The project would languish for days or even weeks if I had unresolved anger in my heart. I just could not bring myself to write about forgiveness in the abstract while denying it in my personal life.

Eventually my problem was resolved when I encountered a statement by Rabbi Isaac Luria (the Arizal), the great Kabbalist and principal student of Rabbi Cordovero. The Arizal taught that each morning one must accept upon one's self the Biblical obligation to "love your fellow as yourself." As an experiment, I began each writing session with a conscious resolve to forgive specific individuals in my life—and suddenly my creative energies expanded, accelerating the completion of manuscript dramatically. Consistency remained elusive—on Tuesday morning I might muster enough forgiveness to write for a full hour, but by Wednesday morning I would discover that my anger and resentment had returned, perhaps not quite as powerfully, but enough to derail my work. Nevertheless, I can state with confidence that if my book succeeds in capturing even a fraction of the lofty ideals of Rabbi Cordovero, it is undoubtedly because the entire work was composed, painfully and fitfully, under the influence of this holy teaching of the Arizal.

Surfside, FL
Adar I 5774 / February 2014

Preface to the Second Edition

In the few short years that passed since *The Kabbalah of Forgiveness* was published, people everywhere have become much kinder and deserving of love and respect. Either that or I have become more forgiving. Both propositions strain credulity, but if I had to choose one over the other, I would hypothesize that the sustained encounter with the holy thought of Rabbi Cordovero has helped me develop spiritual strength in this key area of interpersonal relationships. I hope that this second edition will help you with the same. The second edition differs from the first in a few minor areas, and was occasioned by a request from Ms. Jésica Neuah and Rabbi Abraham Serruyah of Editorial Perspectivas to publish a Spanish-language edition. I am grateful to the kind support of Mr. Sam Sapozhnik, an exceptional individual whose wisdom has guided me at every step.

Cedarhurst, NY

Kislev 5778/December 2017

The Life and Work of Rabbi Moshe Cordovero

Little is known of Rabbi Moshe Cordovero's family background. He was born in 1522 to Yaakov Cordovero; his mother's name and his place of birth are unknown. His surname may indicate that his immediate ancestors were refugees from the Córdoba region of Spain, although his preference for the Portuguese spelling Cordoeiro, as well as his position of authority in the Portuguese Jewish community of Safed, indicate that his family probably migrated to Spain to Portugal at some earlier point, where they may have worked in the maritime industry ("corda" is the Portuguese word for "rope"). and then suffered the Portuguese Expulsion of 1497 before settling in northern Israel. In keeping with widespread convention, we will use the possibly incorrect but popular spelling "Cordovero."

More is known about Rabbi Cordovero's life after his introduction to Kabbalah at the tender age of 20. He was accepted as a student of the renowned kabbalist Rabbi Shlomo Alkabets, a poet who is perhaps best known as the author of the Friday night liturgical poem *Lekha Dodi*. Rabbi Cordovero married Rabbi Alkabets' sister sometime around the beginning of his discipleship. Her name remains unknown. Dr. Zohar Raviv, a noted biographer of Cordovero and specialist in his thought, surmises that the Cordoveros had several children, but only one survived to maturity: Gedalya, who later served as literary executor of his father's works. Rabbi Cordovero died during the plague of 1570 at the age of 48. Gedalyah was eight years old.

Over the course of his short life, Rabbi Cordovero maintained a prodigious literary output. His fame as a Kabbalist was ensured with the appearance of *Pardes*

Rimonim (The Orchard of Pomegranates, 1548), the first truly systematic analysis of Kabbalah. Taking the classical kabbalistic texts from the *Sefer ha-Yetsirah* through the *Zohar*, Rabbi Cordovero provided a comprehensive overview of the major concepts and described a common theoretical foundation for all of them. This work was of such popularity that it was later abbreviated twice for more popular audiences, first by Rabbi Cordovero himself (*Or Ne'erav*, or "The Pleasant Light") and later by his Italian student Menahem Azaria de Fano (known as the Maharam mi-Pano, 1548-1620), who later played an important role in popularizing the work of Rabbi Cordovero. He also wrote kabbalistic commentaries on Biblical texts, the prayer book, and a massive commentary on the *Zohar* entitled *Or Yakar* ("The Precious Light"). While some of his works have been republished several times, the esoteric nature of much of his scholarship meant that few researchers have risen to the task of producing scholarly versions of some of his larger works, including *Eilima Rabati*, much of which remains in manuscript.

Date Palm of Devorah is easily his best-known work. Its appeal extended to an audience far larger than those few initiates in the mysteries of the Kabbalah, and it was disseminated widely by 16th century devotees including Rabbi Levi Horowitz (1565-1630), who included virtually the entire text in his popular magnum opus, the *Shnei Luhot ha-Brit*.

The Safed Moment

The life and work of Rabbi Cordovero is inseparable from the fascinating Golden Age of Safed, a brief period in the 16th century that witnessed a sudden outpouring of Jewish creativity from a small town in the northern Galilee region.

Safed, or *Tsefat* in Hebrew, is not mentioned in the Bible and hardly referred to in the Talmud, and seemed an unlikely place for the profound Jewish renaissance that occurred there, were it not for several factors that contribute to what Dr. Zohar Raviv calls its unique "theography."

The city's name is related to the Hebrew word for "lookout" or "perspective," even "prophecy," and is a fitting descriptor of its location some 800 meters above sea level, looking down on the lush Galilee region and the ancient city of Tiberias. A decline in the local economy of Israel's first city, Jerusalem, combined with policies of the recently installed Ottoman rulers of the region made Safed a magnet for Jewish immigration, particularly those associated with the textile trade. The Safed graves of Rabbis from the Mishnaic period, most notably the father of Jewish mysticism Rabbi Shimon bar Yohai, were magnets for spiritual seekers who made pilgrimage there. In short order the economic potential of the region, combined with its natural beauty and spiritual significance, attracted some of the greatest minds of the 16th century. Many of them were Jewish intellectuals, refugees from the recent expulsions from Spain and Portugal. Rabbi Cordovero's parents or grandparents may have been among them.

It is not known whether Rabbi Cordovero was born in Safed, or, like many, migrated there from Jewish way stations such as Thessaloniki or Istanbul. He was certainly a distinguished student, and became one of the prodigies of none other than Rabbi Yosef Karo (1488-1575), the author of the *Shulhan Arukh*, the Code of Jewish Law. Rabbi Cordovero's intellectual brilliance was immediately recognized by his peers, but contrary to popular belief,

Rabbi Cordovero was probably not included in Rabbi Yaakov Berav's controversial 1538 attempt to renew the ancient process of Biblical ordination (*smikhah*). As Dr. Raviv has amply demonstrated, the notion that the 16-year old Moshe Cordovero would be so honored was an unsubstantiated theory first proposed by 19th century writers, based solely on Rabbi Cordovero's later reputation and contradicted by several salient facts. This is not to say that Rabbi Cordovero did not command great respect for his Talmudic expertise. He served as the head of the Safed Jewish Court (*Bet Din*), and several of his rulings are mentioned in the writings of Rabbi Karo as well. Dr. Raviv characterizes Rabbi Cordovero as more of a lone mystic, occupied with his kabbalistic writings and theories and engaged with his small group of advanced students, participating in communal affairs only when called upon.

Besides his incredibly prolific work as a theorist and writer, Rabbi Cordovero engaged in frequent trips into the forests surrounding Safed, often in the sole company of his teacher, Rabbi Shlomo Alkabets. These excursions, known as *gerushin* ("divorces," or more properly, "exiles") were intended to emulate the feeling of the *Shekhinah*, the Divine Presence, exiled since the dissolution of the Jewish homeland in the 1st century. These *gerushin* should also be understood in the context of the Iberian expulsion, well within generational memory, that were likely felt with the same immediacy that contemporary Jews understand the Holocaust. Together, teacher and student would seek out ancient graves of holy people and meditate there, engaging in deep silent prayers lasting three hours at a time. Rabbi Cordovero described these excursions, and the mystical insights he received during such travels, in a spiritual journal entitled *Sefer Gerushin*, an important work that awaits translation.

Rabbi Cordovero taught many brilliant students, several of whom carried on his legacy with writings of their own, including Rabbi Eliyahu de Vidas (1518-1592), author of *Reishit Hokhmah* ("The Beginning of Wisdom").His most famous student was none other than the great Rabbi Isaac Luria (1534-1572), known as the Arizal, the sole early modern Kabbalist to eclipse Rabbi Cordovero's fame. The Arizal travelled from Egypt to Safed in 1570 to study with Rabbi Cordovero, but their time together was truncated by Rabbi Cordovero's premature passing in 1572. Rabbi Hayim Vital (1543-1620), student to both Rabbi Cordovero and his successor, wrote that despite the brevity of their studies together, the Arizal nevertheless considered Rabbi Cordovero his greatest teacher.

Date Palm of Devorah: A Kabbalistic Approach to Musar

The corpus of Jewish religious literature, from the Bible onward, places great emphasis on the definition of *lawful* behavior and the imperative of *ethical* behavior. Lawful behavior may be understood as the minimum requirement for all Jews, and is subject to reward and punishment. Ethical behavior, on the other hand, is a much more nuanced affair, often reaching far beyond the demands of what is lawful. In other words, legislation concentrates on what one *must* do (that which is lawful), whereas other elements of Jewish thought concentrate on what one *should* do (that which is ethical).

The specific definition of what constitutes lawful behavior is known as *halakhah*, and is fleshed out in texts such as the Mishnah (3rd century), the Talmud (4th-6th centuries) and codified in various compendiums of Jewish law, including the works of Maimonides (12th century). With the possible exception of the 3rd century Mishnaic tractate *Pirkei Avot*, however, most ethical teachings were scattered throughtout these seminal texts, and no single work was exclusively dedicated to the development of ethical sensibility until the Bayha ibn Pakuda of Zaragoza wrote *The Duties of the Heart* in the 11th century. In other words, the trend of defining lawful behavior dominated much Jewish literature for some two millennia, while the more difficult task of understanding the underlying principles of ethical behavior lagged behind. To be sure, general rules such as Hillel's famous dictum, "that which is hateful to you, do not do to your fellow," were studied alongside longer treatments of ethical import in the Talmud and elsewhere, but the beginning of a literary genre devoted specifically to this topic only began much later. This genre is known as *musar* literature.

The term *musar*, derived from the Hebrew term "rebuke" or "test," as well as the term "tradition," was popularized in the late 19th century when Rabbi Israel Lipkin of Salant (Israel Salanter) argued that *musar* study deserved a formal and permanent place in the curriculum of the Yeshivah. Rabbi Salanter maintained that the near-exclusive emphasis on Talmudic studies did not sufficiently expose students of his generation to the introspection and self-analysis required to develop ethical behavior and sustained spiritual growth. His *musar* movement called for renewed effort through the study of a handful of carefully selected works, including *The Duties of the Heart*, *The Ways of the Righteous* by an anonymous 15th century writer, and *The Path of the Just* by Rabbi Moshe Hayim Luzzatto (18th c.). Included in the early canon of *musar* works was our text, *Date Palm of Devorah*.

While all the works of *musar* share the common goal of advancing ethical behavior, they are highly distinct in approach and character. Alan Morinis, a modern proponent of *musar*, identified four distinct tendencies in the literature: the traditional Talmudic approach, seen in the *The Ways of the Righteous*; the philosophical approach, characteristic of Maimonides' *Laws of Opinions*; the ascetic approach, evidenced in the 13th century *Book of the Pious*; and finally the kabbalistic approach, the first and most famous work being Rabbi Moshe Cordovero's *Date Palm of Devorah*.

The principal theme of *Date Palm of Devorah* is the practical application of the concept known among medieval theologians as *imitatio Dei*, or the "imitation of God." This task begins with an underlying, awesome presumption: if we are to somehow imitate God, we must first understand something about God's nature. *Date Palm of Devorah* therefore provides nothing less than a spiritual anatomy of God, insofar as this may be grasped within the parameters of human comprehension. This topic alone would earn it an honored place in the rich history of Jewish spirituality, but the identity of God is merely a precursor to the more relevant task of the book, which is to *apply* this knowledge to our everyday behavior; the concept of *imitatio Dei*. *Date Palm of Devorah* is therefore simultaneously a book of esoteric kabbalistic wisdom as well as a classic of Jewish ethics, and has earned a rare place in the library of *musar* literature.

Published posthumously, the text of *Date Palm of Devorah* contains many unanswered questions. It appears likely that the current text was not the finished version that Rabbi Cordovero intended to publish, as there are a few small errors and omissions that would have been caught with relatively light copyediting. For the most part, these are not major issues. For example, it seems that Rabbi Cordovero composed *Date Palm of Devorah* without ready access to Talmudic texts, relying solely on his prodigious memory. In one instance the text refers the reader to the wrong chapter of Talmud, in another area the name of a Talmudic Rabbi is recorded incorrectly. More seriously, there are some *lacunae* in the work such as a passage in the second chapter which introduces two reasons for a particular phenomenon, but the text only reports one reason. These minor issues have not prevented generations of students from cherishing *Date Palm of Devorah* as a work of soaring genius.

One of the most msysterious aspects of the work is its title, which remains completely unexplained. It is evidently taken from Judges 4:5, and Rabbi Cordovero's son Gedalyah assumed that the title was taken from a section of his father's work *Eilima Rabati*, a book that is divided into sections called "Date Palms." None of those sections are named, however, and a closer examination reveals that, while similar, *Date Palm of Devorah* is clearly distinct from the parallel sixth section of *Eilima Rabati*. It is possible that the text in *Eilima Rabati* was an earlier version of *Date Palm of Devorah* (we do not know with precision when either work was composed), and Rabbi Cordovero decided to develop the ideas more fully in an independent, stand-alone work. *Date Palm of Devorah* may have served as an introduction to his kabbalistic ethical system in the same way that *Or Ne'erav* was written as a separate work to function as an introduction to his Kabbalah as a whole. Dr. Bracha Sack has written extensively on Cordoveran thought, and she suggests that the title may be a reference to the union of husband and wife, a prime and holy physical metaphor for the unity of the Divine Name. A conclusive answer to the mystery of the title may never be found.

The Kabbalah of Forgiveness

Introduction

Date Palm of Devorah begins with an overall statement of purpose: to fully realize human potential, one must master and actualize the concept of *imitatio Dei* (the imitation of God). Two distinct tasks are required. First, the student must understand the nature of God's interaction with the world through the ten *sefirot*, or emanations, through which God created and maintains the Universe (see below for amplification). Second, the student must grasp the manner in which these *sefirot* may be emulated on a human level, which will elicit a parallel and disproportionately beneficial Divine response. The first *sefirah* is *Keter*, the Crown, which is associated with the Thirteen Levels of Mercy. The Thirteen Levels are encoded within a sequence of verses in the prophetic book of Micah (7:18-20). Rabbi Cordovero will use these verses as a framework for a more detailed discussion for the content, meaning, and application of each of the Thirteen Levels.

פֶּרֶק א

הָאָדָם רָאוּי שֶׁיִּדַּמֶּה לְקוֹנוֹ וְאָז יִהְיֶה בְּסוֹד הַצּוּרָה הָעֶלְיוֹנָה צֶלֶם וּדְמוּת, שֶׁאִלּוּ יְדֻמֶּה בְּגוּפוֹ וְלֹא בִּפְעֻלּוֹת הֲרֵי הוּא מַכְזִיב הַצּוּרָה וְיֹאמְרוּ עָלָיו צוּרָה נָאָה וּמַעֲשִׂים כְּעוּרִים. שֶׁהֲרֵי עִיקַּר הַצֶּלֶם וְהַדְּמוּת הָעֶלְיוֹן הֵן פְּעֻלּוֹתָיו, וּמַה יּוֹעִיל לוֹ הֱיוֹתוֹ כְּצוּרָה הָעֶלְיוֹנָה דְּמוּת תַּבְנִית אֵבָרָיו וּבַפְּעֻלּוֹת לֹא יְדֻמֶּה לְקוֹנוֹ.

לְפִיכָךְ רָאוּי שֶׁיִּדַּמֶּה אֶל פְּעֻלּוֹת הַכֶּתֶר שֶׁהֵן י"ג מִדּוֹת שֶׁל רַחֲמִים עֶלְיוֹנוֹת. וּרְמוּזוֹת בְּסוֹד הַפְּסוּקִים מִי אֵל כָּמוֹךָ. יָשׁוּב יְרַחֲמֵנוּ. תִּתֵּן אֱמֶת. אִם כֵּן רָאוּי שֶׁתִּמָּצֶאנָה בּוֹ י"ג מִדּוֹת אֵלּוּ.

וְעַכְשָׁו נְפָרֵשׁ אוֹתָן הַפְּעֻלּוֹת י"ג שֶׁרָאוּי שֶׁתִּהְיֶינָה בּוֹ

Introduction 22

It is Appropriate to Imitate the Creator

It is appropriate to imitate the Creator, and thus participate in the secret of the Supernal Form, Image and Likeness. If a human being were to be similar in external shape, but not in behavior, this would give lie to the Form. People say of such a person, "beautiful in form, but repulsive in behavior." This is because the essence of the Form and Supernal Image is measured in terms of behavior. What benefit is there in participating in the Supernal Form, the very Likeness imprinted on one's limbs, if this similarity to the Creator does not extend to one's conduct as well?

Therefore it is appropriate that we imitate the activity of *Keter*, which consists of the Thirteen Levels of Supernal Mercy, derived from the Biblical passage (Micah 7:18-20): *Who is like You, God, who bears sin and passes over transgression for the remnant of His inheritance. He does not hold fast to His anger forever, for He desires kindness. He will again show mercy, He will subdue our transgressions, and cast all their sins into the depths of the sea. Give truth to Jacob, kindness to Abraham, which You swore to our ancestors from days of old.* Thus it is fitting that a person should develop these Thirteen Levels of Mercy, which we find in the *sefirah* of *Keter*.

Now we will explain the function of the Thirteen Levels as applied to human behavior.

Commentary

In his typically terse and succinct fashion, Rabbi Cordovero introduces the subject of *Date Palm of Devorah*: the kabbalistic approach to *imitatio Dei*, or the "imitation of God." Fulfillment of *imitatio Dei* is central to the meaning of human existence. Made in the image of God, denying our divine potential would represent a betrayal of our fundamental essence, reducing us to something "beautiful in form, but repulsive in behavior." A delicate oil painting may be ripped from its frame and sewn into a very serviceable sack to carry potatoes, but that would constitute an offense to the great beauty of the image painstakingly painted onto the canvas. The same is true of we human beings: infused with the Image of God, we maximize our identity when we bring our conduct into conformity with our Divine potential. "Adam," the Hebrew word for human being, is related to the term *adameh*, which means "I will imitate," as in Isaiah 14:14: *I will imitate* (adameh) *the Most High*.

The concept of imitating God, well developed in the Abrahamic tradition, has its basis in Biblical verses such as Leviticus 19:2: "be holy, for I am holy." Jewish philosophers pondered the implications of this statement: how, precisely, was one to fulfill this awesome requirement, when our transcendent God remains fundamentally unknowable? Rashi, the greatest of the medieval commentators (Rabbi Shlomo Yitshaki, 1040-1105) took a pragmatic approach, writing "cleave to God's ways—perform acts of kindness, bury the dead, visit the sick, just as God did." Maimonides (1135-1204) expounded on the emotional and intellectual implications of *imitatio Dei*, defining the verse "and walk in [God's] ways" (Deuteronomy 28:9) as a form of Aristotelian "Golden Path," finding Godliness in the pursuit of a balanced personality (see *Mishneh Torah,* Hilkhot De'ot and the 14th century *Sefer ha-Hinukh* 611). Rabbi Cordovero's understanding of *imitatio Dei* includes these approaches and surpasses them.

For Rabbi Cordovero, the true meaning of the Biblical phrase "made in the image of God" (Genesis 1:26-27) lies in the appropriate use of the human will. Bringing this will into harmony with God's will represents the maximization of human potential, and is expressed in terms of both behavior and identity, in terms of both action and selfhood. By way of an imperfect analogy, we are like the various wireless devices we use to receive invisible data transmitted through our atmosphere. If our mobile phone is too far away from a cell tower, or if our radio is not tuned to the proper frequency, the signal will be weak or garbled. *Date Palm of Devorah* describes the method of adjusting our spiritual wireless devices to capture the strongest signals. God is constantly broadcasting. We have to work on receiving, and responding.

As long as we fail to bring ourselves into alignment with the Divine signal, we fail to maximize our potential, and are rendered as overqualified for the tasks of life as a computer is overqualified as a doorstop. Rabbi Moshe David Yehezkel Landau provides a memorable image of such underemployment in his commentary on the first chapter of *Date Palm of Devorah.* Imagine a highly trained surgeon, possessing the knowledge and skills to save lives, who takes a job as a cashier in a local grocery store. What a waste of human talent! This is "giving lie to the form," underutilizing the powers locked in the human soul.

The key to *imitatio Dei,* for Rabbi Cordovero, lies in the kabbalistic understanding of how God is revealed in the

Universe through the Divine emanations known as *sefirot* (singular: *sefirah*). These expressions of creative energy are ten in number: *Keter* (the Crown), *Hokhmah* (Wisdom), *Binah* (Understanding), *Hesed* (Kindness), *Gevurah* (Power), *Tiferet* (Glory), *Netsah* (Eternity), *Hod* (Beauty), *Yesod* (Foundation), and *Malkhut* (Sovereignty). *Date Palm of Devorah* goes through the *sefirot* and describes how we may bring our own behavior into precise alignment with each of them, opening up the bandwidth to receive the Divine signal at maximum strength. This book, entitled *The Kabbalah of Forgiveness*, concentrates on the first chapter of *Date Palm of Devorah*, which is dedicated to *Keter* (the Crown). The primary defining characteristic of this *sefirah* is expressed in the Thirteen Levels of Mercy.

Divine Mercy is described in Jewish thought as the *shalosh esrei midot*, which we have rendered here as the Thirteen Levels, although the term Thirteen Attributes would also be correct. God, according to the paucity of our human intellect, utilizes thirteen distinct methods or strategies to effect forgiveness. The Hebrew term *midot* (singular: *midah*) simply translates as "measures," which does not imply that one *midah* is superior to another, but I have chosen to translate this word as "levels," because Rabbi Cordovero's description clearly indicates a progression: the first *midah* is less difficult to achieve than the second, which is in turn less difficult than the third, and so on. On the other hand, sometimes a specific *midah* proves to be the most effective, regardless of the severity of the offense that requires forgiveness: I happen to prefer the first, sixth and thirteenth *midot* over them all, and generally try to focus on them first rather than working through each *midah* in sequence. Rabbi Cordovero advocates this approach in his conclusion: "when one encounters a situation when one needs to employ one of the Levels, let one remember and say 'behold, this matter requires the use of this Level.'"

Thus even though the term "level" reflects the sequential nature of the thirteen, the term "attribute" captures the independent nature of each *midah*. *The Kabbalah of Forgiveness* uses the term Level for consistency, but the reader should bear in mind the dual aspect of the term *midah*.

The Thirteen Levels of Mercy are expressed in two Scriptural passages. The liturgy frequently cites the best-known passage, taken from Exodus 34:6-7: "O Lord, O Lord, compassionate and gracious, patient and full of kindness and truth, who preserves kindness for thousands, who bears transgression and sin and wrong." Prominent in the High Holy Days services, these verses are understood to have tremendous power, as the Talmud describes (*Rosh Hashanah* 17b): "Rabbi Yohanan taught: if it were not stated explicitly, it would be impossible to say this—God wrapped himself as a prayer leader and demonstrated for Moses, saying to him 'any time the Jewish people [sin], let them do the following order [i.e. the Thirteen Levels of Mercy] before me and I will forgive them." Rabbi Eliyahu Vidas, one of Rabbi Cordovero's most famous students, clarifies the meaning of this Talmudic teaching in his classic work *Reishit Hokhmah* ("The Beginning of Wisdom," Gate of Humility 1:14): "we see that many times we recite these Thirteen Levels, and yet we are not answered! The *Geonim* [Rabbis of the late Babylonian period] explain that the phrase 'let them do the following order' does not refer to the wrapping in the prayer shawl [and merely repeating the verses aloud]—it refers rather to the *doing* of these Levels that God taught Moses." The secret to *doing* these Levels, living them and putting them into actual practice, is the subject of *Date Palm of Devorah*.

Besides the formulation in Exodus, The Thirteen Levels of Mercy are also encoded within a few verses in the prophetic book of Micah. The kabbalists draw a distinction between the "lower" version *(seder tata'ah)* that appears most frequently in the liturgy and the "higher" version *(seder ila'ah)* in Micah, which is only recited formally during the *tashlikh* service after Rosh Hashanah. Breaking down several verses into thirteen clauses, the higher version reads as follows (Micah 7:18-20): *(1) Who is like You, God, (2) who bears sin (3) and passes over transgression (4) for the remnant of His inheritance. (5) He does not hold fast to His anger forever, (6) for He desires kindness. (7) He will again show mercy, (8) He will subdue our transgressions and (9) cast all their sins into the depths of the sea. (10) Give truth to Jacob, (11) kindness to Abraham (12) that you swore to our ancestors (13) from days of old.* This formulation of the Thirteen Levels of Mercy is considered higher because it is not placed within the context of a petition. Rather than beseeching God to forgive us our transgressions, a fundamentally retrospective act, the higher version is a description of God's nature, insofar as we may understand it, such that we might engage in *imitatio Dei* and thus elevate our behavior accordingly.

In his commentary on *Date Palm of Devorah*, Rabbi Epstein uses a parable to illustrate the differences between the lower and higher versions of the Thirteen Levels of Mercy. A king may be known in two ways: by the way he rules his people, and the way he behaves alone in his palace. If the king treats his people with mercy and justice, we say he is a merciful and just king, but that is only the outward expression of his inner life in the palace. How does the king think? How does the king conduct himself on his own? This knowledge is reserved only for those who are allowed within the palace to observe the king directly. The lower version of the Thirteen Levels of Mercy, stated as a petition, reflect a lower apprehension of God's nature, perceiving God's majesty like a crowd of peasants standing outside the palace walls, waiting for a royal pronouncement of forgiveness. The higher version, on the other hand, is stated as an expression of praise of God, like a private poem composed by a member of the royal staff, a poem penned by someone who had the opportunity to know the king on a deeper, more personal level, and transform this relationship into a guideline for inspired living. *Date Palm of Devorah* is that poem.

One final note is relevant before we begin the discussion of the Thirteen Levels themselves. Many commentators have been troubled by Rabbi Cordovero's unusual use of the word "appropriate" (ראוי) in the first sentence: "it is *appropriate* to imitate the Creator." They asked, if *imitatio Dei* is a distinct commandment, why is it only "appropriate" to imitate the Creator? Shouldn't Rabbi Cordovero use a term like "mandatory" or "obligated"?

Rabbi Landau offers a powerful image to address the question. He writes that "a person should walk in the street with dignified clothing, and not in pajamas. One need not say 'necessary' or 'obligated' regarding something like this." In other words, while there is no commandment in the Torah that explicitly prohibits the wearing of pajamas in public, such behavior would certainly not fall in the "appropriate" category. The commandment to imitate God has so many nuanced and situation-based practical applications, from one's choice of clothing to one's choice of words, that it would be counterproductive to enumerate them all.

Another possible explanation of the term "appropriate" refers to the overwhelming imperative of forgiveness mandated in *Date Palm of Devorah*, which is of an entirely different order of magnitude than many other commandments. Perhaps Rabbi Cordovero acknowledged the difficulty of the task by using the word "appropriate" rather than "mandatory." The lofty, even otherworldly standards of behavior described in *Date Palm of Devorah* will only be reached by a saintly few. It is appropriate, nevertheless, for the rest of us to at least make the attempt. A son, for example, who wishes to please his father, will certainly pay attention to his father's directions and obey them completely. A son who truly loves his father, on the other hand, will reach beyond the directions in anticipation of the father's deeper intent: "what else can I do for my father? How can I express my respect and love for my father beyond fulfilling his stated requests?"

The commandment of "go in God's ways" (*ve-halakhta be-derakhav*, Deuteronomy 28:9) refers to the more basic, elemental adherence to the explicit teachings of the Torah. The one who truly loves God, however, will reach beyond the commandments to their Source, constantly looking for ways to serve God in a holier, more purified manner. Lofty, detailed, and absolute, the standards of behavior described in the Torah are nevertheless only the minimum requirements. With the opening sentence of *Date Palm of Devorah*, Rabbi Cordovero gently indicates that it is "appropriate" for a person to go beyond the minimum requirements, and seek completely to fulfill the will of our Divine Parent through the application of the Thirteen Levels of Mercy.

The First Level: The King who Endures Insult

Introduction

Rabbi Cordovero's discussion of the Thirteen Levels of Mercy begins with an awesome depiction of human sin from God's perspective.

Given that all power in the Universe has God at its source, even the energy used by human beings in their affairs, it follows that when a person transgresses God's will, he or she inevitably makes use of that very same Divine vitality to rebel against the One who provided it, like a servant who is sent on a mission by his employer, then beats his master with the walking stick he received for that purpose. What a grievous insult! Nevertheless, God endures this insult, and continues to provide life-sustaining energy to human beings, even when they misdirect that energy to do defy God's will.

The first of the Thirteen Levels of Mercy is taken from the beginning of Micah 7:18: Who is like You, God. Rabbi Cordovero outlines the parameters of the first Level, and then indicates some ways in which human beings may emulate Divine forgiveness.

הָאחת - מִי אֵל כָּמוֹךָ

מוֹרֶה עַל הֱיוֹת הָבה"ה מֶלֶךְ נֶעֱלָב, סוֹבֵל עֶלְבּוֹן מַה שֶׁלֹּא יְכִילֵהוּ רַעְיוֹן. הֲרֵי אֵין דָּבָר נִסְתָּר מֵהַשְׁגָּחָתוֹ בְּלִי סָפֵק, וְעוֹד אֵין רֶגַע שֶׁלֹּא יִהְיֶה הָאָדָם נִזּוֹן וּמִתְקַיֵּם מִכֹּחַ עֶלְיוֹן הַשּׁוֹפֵעַ עָלָיו, וַהֲרֵי תִּמְצָא שֶׁמֵּעוֹלָם לֹא חָטָא אָדָם נֶגְדּוֹ שֶׁלֹּא יִהְיֶה הוּא בְּאוֹתוֹ הָרֶגַע מַמָּשׁ שׁוֹפֵעַ עָלָיו שֶׁפַע קִיּוּמוֹ וּתְנוּעַת אֵבָרָיו, וְעִם הֱיוֹת שֶׁהָאָדָם חוֹטֵא בַּכֹּחַ הַהוּא לֹא מְנָעוֹ מִמֶּנּוּ כְּלָל אֶלָּא סָבַל הבה"ה עֶלְבּוֹן כָּזֶה לִהְיוֹת מַשְׁפִּיעַ בּוֹ כֹּחַ תְּנוּעַת אֵבָרָיו, וְהוּא מוֹצִיאָן אוֹתוֹ כֹּחַ בְּאוֹתוֹ רֶגַע בְּחֵטְא וְעָוֹן וּמַכְעִיס וְהבה"ה סוֹבֵל. וְלֹא תֹּאמַר שֶׁאֵינוֹ יָכוֹל לִמְנֹעַ מִמֶּנּוּ הַטּוֹב הַהוּא ח"ו שֶׁהֲרֵי בְּכֹחוֹ בְּרֶגַע כְּמֵימְרָה לְיַבֵּשׁ יָדָיו וְרַגְלָיו כְּעֵין שֶׁעָשָׂה לְיָרָבְעָם, וְעִם כָּל זֹאת שֶׁהַכֹּחַ בְּיָדוֹ לְהַחֲזִיר הַכֹּחַ הַנִּשְׁפָּע הַהוּא וְהָיָה לוֹ לוֹמַר כֵּיוָן שֶׁאַתָּה חוֹטֵא נֶגְדִּי תֶּחֱטָא בְּשֶׁלְּךָ לֹא בְּשֶׁלִּי, לֹא תֶחֱטָא נֶגְדִּי, לֹא מִפְּנֵי זֶה מָנַע טוּבוֹ מִן הָאָדָם אֶלָּא סָבַל עֶלְבּוֹן, וְהִשְׁפִּיעַ הַכֹּחַ וְהֵטִיב לָאָדָם טוּבוֹ. הֲרֵי זֶה עֶלְבּוֹן וְסַבְלָנוּת מַה שֶׁלֹּא ישוער וְעַל זֶה קוֹרְאִים מַלְאֲכֵי הַשָּׁרֵת לְהבה"ה מֶלֶךְ עָלוּב וְהַיְנוּ אוֹמְרוֹ מִי אֵל כָּמוֹךָ, אַתָּה אֵל בַּעַל חֶסֶד הַמֵּטִיב, אֵל בַּעַל כֹּחַ לִנְקֹם וְלֶאֱסֹף אֶת שֶׁלְּךָ, וְעִם כָּל זֹאת אַתָּה סוֹבֵל וְנֶעֱלָב עַד יָשׁוּב בִּתְשׁוּבָה.

הֲרֵי זוֹ מִדָּה שֶׁצָּרִיךְ הָאָדָם לְהִתְנַהֵג בָּהּ רְצוֹנִי הַסַּבְלָנוּת וְכֵן הֱיוֹתוֹ נֶעֱלָב אֲפִלּוּ לְמַדְרֵגָה זוֹ וְעִם כָּל זֹאת לֹא יֶאֱסֹף טוֹבָתוֹ מִן הַמְקַבֵּל:

The First Level

Who is God Like You

This Level demonstrates that God is a King who endures insult to a degree that cannot be imagined. Behold, without doubt nothing is hidden from God's awareness, and there is no moment when a human being is not nourished and sustained by the supernal power that descends from above. Therefore a person never sins against God without simultaneously receiving a sustaining flow of energy from God at the very moment of sin, animating his limbs. Despite the fact that the person uses this energy to sin, God does not withhold it in the least. Rather, God endures this insult and continues to provide the animating life force, even though the person abuses this power to sin, to rebel, and to attempt to anger God—yet God endures the insult.

One cannot say that God does not have the power to withhold this energy from a person, Heaven forbid. God has the power to shrivel a person's hands and feet with a word, as God did with Jeroboam (Kings I 13:4). Despite the fact that God has the power to reverse this flow of energy, saying, "Since you sin against Me—sin with your own power and not Mine," God nevertheless does not withhold this benefit; rather, God endures the insult and continues to send the flow of power, providing him with God's goodness. Behold, this is a level of insult and tolerance that cannot be described.

This is why the ministering angels refer to God as the Insulted King. This is the meaning of "Who is God like You." You are a God of kindness and generosity, a God with the power to take vengeance and take back what is Yours, yet You show tolerance to insult until the person repents.

Behold, this is a Level that one must emulate, meaning: tolerance. We must tolerate insult even to this degree and not retract the benefits we give to others.

Commentary

The concept of the King who endures insult (literally, the "Insulted King," *Pirkei Heikhalot* 25) is one of the most powerful images in *Date Palm of Devorah*. Rabbi Cordovero does not mean that God is somehow upset by this insult, as the anthropomorphism of Divine emotion is used only to provide understanding on a human level. In other words, God is not really insulted, but we behave in a shamefully insulting manner.

God is the sole source of energy in this world, abundant and generous, and without this flow of divine energy nothing at all may exist. As human beings, we are given the discretion of how to use that energy, for good or for ill, yet if we choose to employ it in a forbidden manner we thereby cause great insult to the King. The amazing aspect of this Level is that God does not withhold the supply of this energy, even when we misdirect it to forbidden purposes. The Midrash describes a telling example of this Level (*Tanhuma*, Ki Tisa 14): when the Sea of Reeds was split to allow the Jews to escape from their Egyptian pursuers, a group of Jews insisted on bringing an idol along with them through the parted waters. Even at the very moment that God was providing for their rescue, these Jews insisted on maintaining an attachment to that which God abhors! Similarly, the Midrash continues, when the Jews were sustained in the desert by the miraculous manna, some Jews set aside loaves to provide offerings to the golden calf.

God would be entirely within the boundaries of common morality to cause an immediate end to these essential services, as in the case of King Jeroboam, whose arm was frozen in place when he sought to worship an idol. God could have withdrawn the power that held the waters in place, allowing the waves to crash down upon the fleeing Jews, for example, or God could have ceased sending the flow of manna from Heaven—yet the King who endures insult tolerated this provocation and continued to provide for the Jewish people. In fact, as Rabbi Eliyahu Dessler observes (*Mikhtav mi-Eliyahu* 3:69, cited by several commentators), our intransigence even makes God an unwilling partner in the transgression: by allowing us the energy to sin, God is forced to participate in our wrongdoing. Rather than limit the extent of our free will, however, God endures the insult, overlooking the respect and compliance that we, by all rights, owe in gratitude for our very lives.

The Talmud puts this Level in another way (*Megilah* 31): "where you find God's greatness, there you will find God's humility." In another passage (*Yoma* 69), Moses is criticized by later prophets for the terminology used in prayer: "Moses came and said, 'the God who is Great, and Mighty, and Awesome.' Jeremiah came and said, 'foreigners are dancing in the sanctuary [of the destroyed Temple], where is God's Awesomeness?' Moses removed 'Awesome.' Daniel came and said, 'foreigners are subjugating God's children, where is God's Might?' Moses removed 'Mighty.' The Men of the Great Assembly [who finalized the text of the liturgy] came and said, 'on the contrary—this is God's Might, for God's overwhelming Mercy grants patience to the wicked. This is the Might and Awesomeness of the Blessed One.'"

Perhaps the easiest way to imagine this Level in human terms is by contemplating the relationship between a parent and an adolescent child. Speaking as a father of six, I have some personal knowledge of the trials of tolerance my wife and I endure as we navigate our sons and daughters through the difficult time when they were no longer children, yet not quite adults. As reasonably responsible and loving parents, we devoted ourselves to providing them with the resources they needed to grow to healthy independence, resources material, moral, and spiritual. From the moment each of our precious children was born, we made the acquisition and distribution of such resources one of life's highest priorities. Yet it often takes years, even decades, for a child to realize the enormity of self-sacrifice that parents shoulder without complaint. During that dark time of adolescent ignorance and rebellion, even the most adoring and loving child may say hurtful things and make harmful choices that pain a parent, yet the parent nevertheless continues to provide for the child, hoping that at some point the child will mature and behave in a healthy and productive manner.

The symmetry of the parent-child and God-human relationship, however striking, is only one example of the type of relationship affected by the First Level of Mercy; relationships that have at their essence a kindness extended by one party that is not adequately appreciated by the other. The principle of enduring insult may be applied to the employer who tolerates an ungrateful employee, or the spouse who perseveres without thanks through trying times in a marriage. There are limits to such behaviors, although Rabbi Cordovero does not discuss explicitly them in *Date Palm of Devorah,* and especially not in this section which deals exclusively with the *sefirah* of *Keter*. Disciplining a child, censuring an employee and severing a relationship have their places in Jewish law, but the task outlined in the first chapter of *Date Palm of Devorah* is forgiveness, not justice. The theme of the sixth chapter, based on the Attribute of *Gevurah* (Power), explores that aspect of human relationships.

The First Level of Mercy speaks to us on a human level, perhaps because nothing seems to hurt as much as being underappreciated. When we feel hurt in this manner, Rabbi Cordovero urges us to pause and reflect on the tolerance of the King who endures insult and refrain from responding until the pain is dissipated. It may be worthwhile and appropriate to communicate our feelings, but expressing them may provoke a defensive reaction that compounds the problem rather than alleviating it. We do not have the infinite patience of the King who endures insult, but we can at least try to wait a day or two before raising the issue with the one who offended us. We may even be able to rise above the pain, which is a highly valued element of spiritual growth. At the very least we will be able to choose an approach that will minimize the confrontation.

Date Palm of Devorah, despite its slim profile, can be an overwhelming work. Thirteen different Levels of Mercy can be difficult to process and assimilate, especially on the first reading. To assist the reader who seeks to understand fully the thirteen different methods of forgiveness outlined in *Date Palm of Devorah*, it may be helpful to consider the following theoretical scenarios in which the First Level may be applied in daily life.

Practical Applications

Leah is standing in the express check-out line at the local grocery store. A sign prominently displays the restrictions of this lane: maximum 10 items. She has been waiting for a while, and no one is behind her. A pleasant woman approaches Leah with a smile and asks if she may take her place in line because she is in a hurry to get home. Leah is also in a hurry to get home, but she has been reading *Date Palm of Devorah,* so she graciously gestures that the woman may proceed ahead of her. As Leah congratulates her for her exceptional kindness, she notes that the woman has an unusually large number of items in her basket, and Leah counts them on the conveyor belt—eighteen items! Well over the maximum number allowed for this express lane! How dare she take advantage of Leah's generosity by flouting the rules of the express lane, requiring Leah to wait almost double the time it would take if she had limited herself to only ten items? Nevertheless, Leah remembers the King who Endures Insult—God provides energy to sustain us even when we use it in a rebellious manner—and Leah decides to allow the woman to continue without protest. Well done.

Samuel's adolescent son shows disrespect and ingratitude. Thinking of the King who Endures Insult, Samuel remembers that this rebellion is part of the maturation process. Samuel works to remove anger and hurt from his heart, and uses discretion when imposing consequences, choosing a reprimand that will help the child appreciate Samuel's constant love and support while also avoiding punishments that will increase the alienation between him and his son. Samuel strives to always allow his son a fair opportunity to redeem himself and avoid the consequence, remembering that the point of the punishment is not to aggrieve the child, rather, it is to help him grow spiritually and develop a healthy independence.

Avraham read *Date Palm of Devorah* and wants to be proactive, developing his ability to forgive so that he will be ready when the trial comes. In order to do so, he practices freely devoting his time, energy and finances in an unconditional manner, mentally preparing himself to give without expecting gratitude in return. It's a daunting exercise, but he begins with a small project: he identifies three friends he hasn't spoken to in a long time, and writes them old-fashioned paper letters. He mails them without expecting a response.

The Second Level: Let it Go for Now

The second of the Thirteen Levels, "Who Bears Sin," describes a degree of mercy that is even more profound than the previous Level. In the Second Level, Rabbi Cordovero outlines the metaphysical consequence of sin: with every hurtful act, a negative entity is created, a kind of energy debt that demands payment from its human creator. This being, called a "prosecutor" or "destroyer" in Rabbinic literature, affixes itself like a spiritual leech to the person who made it, and requires an energy source to maintain its existence. Were the prosecutor to draw its vitality from its human source, the results would be disastrous for the person who created the being through his or her transgression. The Second Level of Mercy demonstrates how God overlooks the fact that the prosecutor was born from an act of rebellion against God's will, and directs the prosecutor to delay exacting its due from the human. Just as we saw in the First Level of Mercy, in which God continued to provide energy to people despite their wrongful deeds, in the Second Level, God even provides energy to the prosecutors, stepping in and providing life-giving forbearance until the human being may address the debt of sin in an appropriate fashion.

The Kabbalistic content of *Date Palm of Devorah* deepens with the Second Level, yet Rabbi Cordovero nevertheless concludes with a discussion of the human applications of the principles inherent in "Who Bears Sin."

הַשֵּׁנִית - נוֹשֵׂא עָוֹן

וַהֲרֵי זֶה גָּדוֹל מֵהַקֹּדֶם שֶׁהֲרֵי לֹא יַעֲשֶׂה הָאָדָם עָוֹן שֶׁלֹּא יִבְרָא מַשְׁחִית כְּדִתְנַן הָעוֹשֶׂה עֲבֵרָה אַחַת קָנָה לוֹ קַטֵגוֹר אֶחָד וַהֲרֵי אוֹתוֹ קַטֵגוֹר עוֹמֵד לִפְנֵי הב"ה וְאוֹמֵר פְּלוֹנִי עֲשָׂאַנִי, וְאֵין בְּרִיָּה מִתְקַיֶּמֶת בָּעוֹלָם אֶלָּא בְּשִׁפְעוֹ שֶׁל הב"ה וַהֲרֵי הַמַּשְׁחִית הַזֶּה עוֹמֵד לְפָנָיו וּבַמֶּה מִתְקַיֵּם.

הַדִּין נוֹתֵן שֶׁיֹּאמַר הב"ה אֵינִי זָן מַשְׁחִיתִים יֵלֵךְ אֵצֶל מִי שֶׁעֲשָׂאוֹ וְיִתְפַּרְנֵס מִמֶּנּוּ וְהָיָה הַמַּשְׁחִית יוֹרֵד מִיָּד וְנוֹטֵל נִשְׁמָתוֹ אוֹ כוֹרְתוֹ אוֹ נֶעֱנָשׁ עָלָיו כְּפִי עָנְשׁוֹ עַד שֶׁיִּתְבַּטֵּל הַמַּשְׁחִית הַהוּא, וְאֵין הב"ה עוֹשֶׂה כֵן אֶלָּא נוֹשֵׂא וְסוֹבֵל הֶעָוֹן וּכְמוֹ שֶׁהוּא זָן הָעוֹלָם כֻּלּוֹ זָן וּמְפַרְנֵס הַמַּשְׁחִית הַזֶּה עַד שֶׁיִּהְיֶה אֶחָד מִשְּׁלֹשָׁה דְּבָרִים, אוֹ שֶׁיָּשׁוּב הַחוֹטֵא בִּתְשׁוּבָה וִיאַכִּילֵהוּ וִיבַטְּלֵהוּ בְּסִגּוּפָיו, אוֹ יְבַטְּלֵהוּ שׁוֹפֵט צֶדֶק בְּיִסּוּרִים וּמִיתָה, אוֹ יֵלֵךְ בַּגֵּיהִנֹּם וְשָׁם יִפְרַע חוֹבוֹ. וְהַיְנוּ שֶׁאָמַר קַיִן גָּדוֹל עֲוֹנִי מִנְּשׂוֹא וּפֵרְשׁוּ רַז"ל כָּל הָעוֹלָם כֻּלּוֹ אַתָּה סוֹבֵל יְרַצֶּה זָן וּמְפַרְנֵס, וַעֲוֹנִי כָּבֵד שֶׁאֵין אַתָּה יָכוֹל לְסוֹבְלוֹ פֵּרוּשׁ לְפַרְנְסוֹ עַד שֶׁאָשׁוּב וַאֲתַקֵּן.

אִם כֵּן הֲרֵי זֶה מִדַּת סַבְלָנוּת גְּדוֹלָה שֶׁיָּזוּן וּמְפַרְנֵס

בְּרִיָּה רָעָה שֶׁבָּרָא הַחוֹטֵא עַד שֶׁיָּשׁוּב.

יִלְמֹד הָאָדָם כַּמָּה צָרִיךְ שֶׁיִּהְיֶה סַבְלָן לִסְבֹּל עַל חֲבֵרוֹ וְרָעוֹתָיו שֶׁהֵרִיעַ לוֹ עַד שִׁעוּר כָּזֶה שֶׁעֲדַיִן רָעָתוֹ קַיֶּמֶת, שֶׁחָטָא נֶגְדּוֹ וְהוּא יִסְבֹּל עַד יְתַקֵּן חֲבֵרוֹ אוֹ עַד שֶׁיִּתְבַּטֵּל מֵאֵלָיו וְכַיּוֹצֵא:

The Second Level

Who Bears Sin

This Level is greater than the First Level, for behold, a person does not transgress without creating a destroyer, as it is taught, "One who commits a specific transgression acquires a specific prosecutor." This prosecutor stands before God and says, "he made me!" Since no creature in the universe can exist without receiving energy from God, then how can this destroyer be sustained when it too stands before God?

It would be reasonable for God to say, "I do not sustain destroyers—go to the one who created you, and take your sustenance from him!" The destroyer would then immediately go down and take the person's life, or excise him, or otherwise punish him until that destructive force would be neutralized. God does not do this. Instead, God bears and tolerates the sin, just as God sustains the entire world. God continues to feed and sustain this destroyer until one of three things happen: either the sinner repents, thus destroying and nullifying the destroyer with his self-affliction, or the True Judge nullifies it through the suffering and death of the sinner, or the sinner goes to *Gehinnom* and there fulfills his debt. This is the meaning of what Cain said: *is my sin too great to bear?* The Rabbis explained this to mean, "You tolerate the entire world," meaning feeding and sustaining Creation. "Is my sin so heavy, that You cannot bear it?" Meaning, can You not sustain it as well, until I may repent and repair the damage?

Thus this is a great Level of tolerance, that God feeds and sustains the evil creature that the sinner created until the sinner repents.

A person should learn the necessity of tolerance, enduring offense from others and whatever harm they caused. Even when the harm persists, one should be patient and allow a person to repair the damage or wait until it resolves of its own accord, and so on.

Commentary

Rabbi Cordovero's understanding of the passage in *Pirkei Avot* 4:13 ("one who commits a specific transgression acquires a specific prosecutor") is quite literal. Committing an ugly act releases negative energy into the world. This negative energy, called a "prosecutor" (*k'tegor*) is also what Rabbi Cordovero calls a "destroyer" (*mashkhit*) and the 19th century Lithuanian Kabbalist Rabbi Hayim of Volozhin calls a "negative angel" (*malakh shelili*). It constitutes a definite spiritual entity with some level of self-consciousness and the power to harm. Ironically, the creation of such harmful beings is the negative aspect of kabbalistic *imitatio Dei* itself, as explained by Rabbi Hayim of Volozhin: just as we are able to elicit divine power through imitating God's Thirteen Levels of Mercy, we also have the power, Heaven forbid, to unleash incredible destruction through the creation of entities made of negative energy.

This concept, though profoundly mystical, is nevertheless part of the commonplace education of Jewish children in observant homes, who are often taught the positive side of this equation when parents urge them to perform various good deeds. A child is encouraged to clearly articulate blessings before eating food, for example, because this act will create a powerful angel (*malakh*) that will improve the very cosmos, and will always be credited to its creator, a small child. The negative aspect of the physics of transgression, however, is also true. Harmful or hateful acts create harmful, hateful beings, and they are likewise associated with the person who created them.

This destructive force may be understood as a type of negative integer, a kind of vacuum created by the absence of holiness. For example, if Reuben commits some type of transgression, perhaps speaking ill of Shimon behind his back, this creates a destructive force with a certain level of power. To assign an arbitrary number, let's assume this wrong generates three units of negative energy, enough to permanently harm a friendship but not enough to dissolve a strong marriage. Left to its own devices, this force may roam the world, wreaking havoc whenever it can, adhering to people, places and things whenever possible, although it remains spiritually tethered to its human source. In his erudite and deeply kabbalistic commentary to *Date Palm of Devorah*, Rabbi Mordechai Shaynberg writes that this energy is invisible to us while our souls are yet in our bodies, and is revealed only at the moment of death as illustrated in the Talmudic teaching (*Berakhot* 6b), "if our eyes were able to see, we would go mad for all the destroyers that surround us." Moreover, continues Rabbi Shaynberg, the sustenance of these beings is destruction itself: they feed on suffering.

Like all created beings, this destroyer also requires a regular infusion of Divine energy to maintain its existence. Let's assume this *mashkhit* requires one unit per year. According to the property of the Second Level, God "bears sin" and provides that unit of energy without fail, year after year, hoping that Reuben will eventually address it himself. Ultimately, however, that energy deficit (the three units assessed at the moment the *mashkhit* is created, plus the accumulated yearly units that build up as long as the *mashkhit* exists) will have to be reconciled. So operates the physics of transgression. Rabbi Cordovero, echoing Maimonides, describes three mechanisms that will neutralize the negative being, all of which involve suffering. Either the debt is paid through the release of energy at the moment of Reuben's death, or by a reduction of the amount of Divine energy allotted to Reuben (this is the meaning of "excision," or *karet*, a punishment that has horrible consequences), or through this-worldly payment through suffering. Of the three, punishment in this world is considered optimal.

This is the sense of Cain's question in Genesis 4:13, as expanded in the Midrash (*Tanhuma* 10:9). He realized the profundity of his evil act of fratricide and the awesomely powerful nature of the *mashkhit* he created through that first, horrible act of human violence. He begged God to allow him an easier way to eliminate that negative energy, but God was unwilling—the vacuum of holiness created by this murder would be addressed only through his suffering. This is much like a homeowner who defaults on loan payments, and asks forbearance from the bank in order to have more time to pay off a huge debt. The bank may refuse, creating significant hardship for the borrower, even homelessness.

Rabbi Epstein takes pains to note, however, that we may often determine the specific type of suffering we endure to eliminate our prosecutors: the essential point of the Second Level of Forgiveness is that God gives us time to refinance our spiritual debt, restructuring the payments in a manner that we can manage successfully. He cites a Midrash from the Talmud (*Avodah Zarah* 4), "a man owes money to two other men, one who is his friend and one who is his enemy. The friend takes payment little by little, while the enemy demands immediate payment in full." God takes over our regular payments on the debt of sin—God does not pay it off, leaving us to deal with it, but through the Second Level of Mercy, God gives us time to get our spiritual finances in order and pay off our debts with dignity.

We should not think, however, that we are trapped in a vortex of suffering punishments for the fleeting pleasures of transgressions. Like a parent of a misbehaving adolescent, God does not seek to exact penalties for our misdeeds simply in order to maintain a metaphysically balanced budget of sins versus good deeds. Rather, in the words of the Prophet Ezekiel (33:11), "Say to them, 'by My life, says the Lord God, I do not desire the death of the wicked, but that he turn from his way and live. Return, return from your evil ways—why die, Jewish people?" God wants us to do *teshuvah*, "return," and become more perfect human beings. We must expend energy to dissipate the energy vacuum of the destroyer, but we have the power to choose the type of energy required for *teshuvah*: regret, confession, and a firm commitment to abandon the negative behavior pattern. If our crimes merit the spiritual death penalty, then through *teshuvah* perhaps we may exempt ourselves through the solitary confinement of deep introspection. If they merit imprisonment, perhaps we may elect to fulfill our obligation through mandatory community service of kindness to others. If they merit financial penalty, perhaps we may make good our debt through expending our resources in charitable contributions. Above them all, continues Rabbi Epstein following the teachings of Rabbi Hayim of Volozhin, is the value of Torah study, which inspires not only greater levels of *teshuvah*, but more importantly, "study leads to action" (*Kidushin* 40b).

The Second Level of Mercy teaches much about the relationship between humans and God, but the principal task of *Date Palm of Devorah* is the translation of this new understanding to interpersonal relationships between human beings. God has the power to take on the energy debt of the destroyer, but is it possible for a human being to do the same for another person? And even if it were possible, would it be appropriate? Rabbi Cordovero does not address this question in *Date Palm of Devorah*, but Rabbi Landau comments on the ways in which we may nevertheless emulate the Second Level of Mercy in our everyday life. We are not required, he writes, to sustain the spiritual products of other people's transgressions; we are only asked to tolerate them, giving others the opportunity to address their wrongs on their own. Note that this only applies to spiritual damage, not actual physical harm, as described on a *halakhic* or legal level. Should Reuben, for example, set a fire on his own property, and it spreads to his neighbor's property, Shimon is obligated to take measures to prevent further damage to the neighbor's land, regardless of Reuben's failure to respond. In other words, we are not required to allow physical damage to increase (even though God may allow this as a consequence of the exercise of human free will). Our challenge, as defined by the *imitatio Dei* inherent in the Second Level of Mercy, is primarily in the area of character. We must show forbearance and allow people to grow spiritually at their own pace. As Rabbi Israel Salanter once put it, "most people are concerned with their own material situation, and other people's spiritual situation, when they really should be concerned with their own spiritual situation, and other people's material situation." It is incumbent upon us to allow others to address the spiritual failings when they are ready, giving them the opportunity to advance at their own pace. The following practical applications provide some suggestions on how the Second Level of Mercy may be put into practice.

Practical Applications

Levi pulls into the parking lot at work and sees that Judah has parked in his spot. Again. Judah knows this is Levi's assigned spot, not so close to the door but at least it's not under the tree that drops its sticky buds all over his white car. Levi parks elsewhere, enters the office and presents himself at Judah's cubicle. Judah's on the phone, and without looking at Levi, he raises his finger to indicate that he's busy and will get to him when he can. At this point Levi is infuriated, and his first thought is to walk to his desk and immediately call the towing company, but Levi takes a deep breath and thinks of the Second Level of Mercy, and decides to give Judah time to address his wrong. Levi pulls out a post-it note, writes "please move your car to your assigned spot," and leaves it on Judah's computer monitor. He then congratulates himself on successfully implementing the Second Level, giving Judah time to right his wrong (advanced students might even write "please park your car in your assigned spot tomorrow," giving Judah a full day to deal with the problem, but that may be too taxing).

Miriam held her head in both hands as she tried to negotiate a way through the bills scattered across the dining room table. No matter how much she tried, there never seemed to be enough money to keep the rent paid, lights on, and food in the refrigerator every month. With painfully meticulous budgeting she came close, but this was too much: a speeding ticket she received while rushing to get her sister to her appointment. How was she going to find another $100 to take care of this flimsy yellow paper? The worst part of it all was that her sister seemed completely oblivious to her role in the whole affair—late getting ready, demanding nevertheless that she arrive on time, and arguing all the way there, even criticizing her in front of the policeman!

Thankfully, Miriam has been studying *Date Palm of Devorah*, and she sees this as an opportunity to exercise the Second Level of Forgiveness. The ticket was created, at least in part, by her sister's behavior, and she shows no signs of accepting responsibility. Miriam could demand that she pay something toward the ticket (not to mention the rent, the groceries, the electricity, etc.) but she knows that her sister's income is almost nil. Miriam therefore takes a deep breath, sets aside her anger and frustration, and writes a check for the ticket. One day her sister will recognize everything Miriam has done for her, but for now, she will continue to thanklessly bear the burden of helping out her out.

Isaac, reading *Date Palm of Devorah*, wants to proactively develop the ability to forgive people in accordance with the Second Level of Mercy. He picks up his phone and goes through all his old contacts, thinking to himself: how do I feel about this person? Suddenly he comes to Joseph, and remembers their harsh parting some years ago. Isaac realizes he harbors much resentment for Joseph over that incident at the Stein wedding. As he reflects on the argument they had, he realizes two things: first, the passage of time has quelled his anger and he feels he can look back at the situation more rationally now, and second, he realizes with dismay that Joseph may actually have been right all along. Grimacing, Isaac understands that he acted like an idiot, and ruined a great friendship that night.

Isaac started this mental exercise looking for someone to forgive, and ended up discovering that he needed forgiveness himself. He wondered if Joseph still bore hard feelings for him, and decided that there was only one way to find out, and only one way to repair their relationship. He pressed the call button and held the phone to his ear, waiting for his friend to pick up.

The Third Level: Take Care of It Personally

Introduction

The Third Level of Mercy addresses the personal role that God plays in the process of forgiveness. Rather than relying on an angel or some other intermediary to dispense clemency, God personally provides the cleansing pardon.

The commentators on *Date Palm of Devorah* expand the Kabbalistic context of this Level, answering the obvious question: why does God personally provide forgiveness, when in virtually all other aspects of the functioning of the Universe, God assigns myriads upon myriads of angels to carry out their delegated tasks? What is special about forgiveness, that it requires the personal intervention of the Master of the Universe?

The answer lies in very structure of the cosmos, and the nature of human power. According to the Kabbalah, the Universe is actually four distinct worlds, in descending order: *atsilut, beriah, yetsirah,* and *asiyah*. Human beings, made in the image of God, have the power to create entities, for good or evil, as discussed above in the Second Level. These entities may be rooted in the three lower worlds, but they cannot penetrate the highest world of *atsilut*. The angels, not created in the image of God, do not have the power to destroy the negative energy beings created through human sin. Only God, who controls all the worlds, can remove these negative beings (or in some cases, even transform them into positive beings), and thus the task of forgiveness is undertaken by God alone.

Rabbi Cordovero briefly alludes to a powerful metaphor to illustrate the human application of the Second Level of forgiveness: the mother who washes a child that has soiled himself.

הַשְּׁלִישִׁית - וְעוֹבֵר עַל פֶּשַׁע

זוֹ מִדָּה גְדוֹלָה שֶׁהֲרֵי אֵין הַמְּחִילָה עַל יְדֵי שָׁלִיחַ אֶלָּא עַל יָדוֹ מַמָּשׁ שֶׁל הַבּ"ה כְּדִכְתִיב כִּי עִמְּךָ הַסְּלִיחָה וְגוֹ' וּמַה הִיא הַסְּלִיחָה שֶׁהוּא רוֹחֵץ הֶעָוֹן כְּדִכְתִיב אִם רָחַץ ה' אֵת צֹאַת בְּנוֹת צִיּוֹן וְגוֹ' וְכֵן כְּתִיב וְזָרַקְתִּי עֲלֵיכֶם מַיִם טְהוֹרִים וְגוֹ' וְהַיְינוּ וְעוֹבֵר עַל פֶּשַׁע שׁוֹלֵחַ מֵימֵי רְחִיצָה וְעוֹבֵד וְרוֹחֵץ הַפֶּשַׁע.

וְהִנֵּה מַמָּשׁ כִּדְמוּת זֶה צָרִיךְ לִהְיוֹת הָאָדָם שֶׁלֹּא יֹאמַר וְכִי אֲנִי מְתַקֵּן מַה שֶּׁפְּלוֹנִי חָטָא אוֹ הִשְׁחִית, לֹא יֹאמַר כָּךְ שֶׁהֲרֵי הָאָדָם חוֹטֵא וְהַבּ"ה בְּעַצְמוֹ שֶׁלֹּא עַל יְדֵי שָׁלִיחַ מְתַקֵּן אֶת מְעֻוָּתוֹ וְרוֹחֵץ צֹאַת עֲוֹנוֹ.

וּמִכָּאן יִתְבַּיֵּשׁ הָאָדָם לָשׁוּב לַחֲטֹא שֶׁהֲרֵי הַמֶּלֶךְ בְּעַצְמוֹ רוֹחֵץ לִכְלוּךְ בְּגָדָיו:

The Third Level

And Passes Over Transgression

This is a great Level, for behold, forgiveness is not granted through a messenger, rather directly by God, as it is written: *for with You is forgiveness.* What is this forgiveness? God washes away the transgression, as it is written: *God washes away the filth of the children of Zion,* and it is written: *I will sprinkle upon you pure waters.* "Passing over transgression" indicates that God sends the cleansing water, and personally washes away sin.

A person must act in precisely this way. One should not say, "Should I be the one to fix whatever wrong this other person caused, or address whatever damage he incurred?" One should not speak in this manner! Behold, when a human being sins, God personally straightens what is bent and washes away the filth of the transgression.

From this we learn that one should be ashamed to return to his sin, for behold, the

King personally washes the dirt off his clothing.

Commentary

The key phrase in this Level is the proof text Rabbi Cordovero quotes from Psalm 130: *for with You is forgiveness.* Forgiveness comes personally and directly from God, and not from some other intermediary. God does not summarily dismiss the penitent, who is grateful but still mired in the aftereffects of the original transgression. On the contrary, God takes a personal and direct interest in the cleansing of the wrongdoer.

The Hebrew word used in Isaiah 4:4 for "filth" above is צואה, literally "excrement," a byproduct of human existence that is at once repulsive and necessary. God acts, as Rabbi Goldberg puts it in his commentary, like a mother who washes a young son who has soiled himself. This powerful image is alluded to with the proof text from Ezekiel 36:25 above. I imagine a child of six or seven, old enough to be toilet-trained yet liable to have an accident, and equally unable properly to cleanse himself of his own excrement. He relies on the kindness of his mother to render him clean and healthy. His beloved mother forgoes her own dignity and personally washes off his defiled body, removing all trace of the offending material. She does this without a word of chastisement—on the contrary, she appreciates the humiliation of her son and performs this task with a smile. Imagine his gratitude and his profound understanding of the depth of her kindness and love for him!

On a mystical level, this Level follows logically from the previous Level. The negative energy generated by sin must have an anchor to the person who created it, just as a leech creates a bit of open skin to attach to its host. Even once the leech is removed and destroyed, the wound at the point of contact must be cleansed and healed or infection will set in. Like a compassionate nurse, God personally sanitizes the lesion on the soul, removing the harmful bacteria of sin and restoring the penitent to health.

Rabbi Epstein, also taking a Kabbalistic approach, describes the cleansing process in an entirely different manner. Citing the Rabbinic proverb, "one who defiles himself below—they defile him from above," Rabbi Epstein attributes the unnamed "they" to the destroyers originally created by the wrongdoing of a person. The "above" refers to the three lower worlds (*beriah*, *yetsirah* and *asiyah*), where these prosecutors live, exerting their negative energy drain on the human being that created them. No matter how consequential the transgression, however, a human being does not have the power to create a destroyer that can penetrate the highest world of *atsilut*. (This is not the case with a being created through an act of kindness, as we shall see in Level Six: such beings are allowed entry even into the highest world.) While human beings have the power to create the prosecutors, they do not have the power to destroy them, especially those who exist on the plane of *beriah*. Only God, who controls all the worlds, can remove these harmful creatures.

This power of "passing over transgression" may be understood by way of analogy. I share my personal laptop computer at home with my children, giving them each a distinct login identity. From time to time, however, they may inadvertently do harm to the computer, changing the settings to the screen resolution or even downloading a virus from the Internet. If they cannot fix the problem themselves, they present me with the laptop, because I have a superior level of power over the computer through my "Administrator Password." With my higher authority, I can fix anything from a forgotten password to the complete removal of a problematic program. Similarly, we may feel that our sins have created so many destroyers that we cannot possibly eliminate them through repentance, but this is not the case. God possesses the Administrator Password to all existence, and if we approach God with our problems, God can easily remove whatever harm we inflicted on the cosmos.

Rabbi Goldberg points out a serious caveat to this Level: it refers to a person who repents out of love (*teshuvah me-ahavah*), in contrast to one who merely repents out of fear (*teshuvah me-yirah*). When a person sincerely repents of wrongdoing and wishes to get closer to God in the process, then God becomes personally involved and helps the penitent address the underlying causes for the transgression, wiping away the filth and leaving the person unsullied and renewed. If, on the other hand, the person repents merely out of fear of punishment, God does not necessarily use the Third Level, forgiving the transgression itself (for there was some element of repentance) but not investing further energy into the deeper motivation for the sin.

Rabbi Shaynberg, on the other hand, disagrees with Rabbi Goldberg's reading of the Third Level. He argues that God provides this forgiveness even to one who repents out of the fear of punishment. Ultimately, he writes, if the penitent has completely resolved never to repeat the harmful behavior, this will invoke the cleansing process of forgiveness. Citing Rabbi Avraham Galante (d. 1560), Rabbi Shaynberg asserts that tears of regret have the power to elicit the Third Level. When a person sincerely laments his or her past behavior and sheds bitter tears of remorse, these human "waters" awaken the Divine "waters" of forgiveness mentioned in the verse from Ezekiel 36:25: *and I will sprinkle upon you pure waters.*

The distinction between the efficacy of repentance out of love (*teshuvah me-ahavah*) and repentance out of fear (*teshuvah me-yirah*) relates to the perspective of the one who has become soiled with transgression, and this topic will be continued later in Level Seven. The goal of *Date Palm of Devorah*, however, is to deepen our understanding of God's perspective, such that we may improve our own attitudes and behaviors. Rabbi Cordovero therefore urges us to take a Divine approach to the sins of others. Just as God will exert Divine power to wash away the filth, even when the defilement is completely the result of a person's rebellious transgression, so too should we undertake to assist another with the damage that he or she has created. We should not unthinkingly say, "why should I help? Let him clean up his own mess!" Such an attitude does not absolve the wrongdoer of responsibility, and depending on the context we may have to qualify our assistance, perhaps with an appropriately gentle rebuke or with a clearly stated limitation of our assistance.

With children, for example, it may be more beneficial in the long run to have a child address at least some of the consequences, in order that he or she may understand the meaning of whatever wrong they caused.

When I was a child of six or seven, I encouraged two neighborhood boys to shoplift some matchbox cars from the local hardware store, thinking that even if they were caught, I would be held blameless. They were, and I wasn't. To teach me a lesson my father drove me to the Ontario Provincial Police station and had me interview with the constable on duty and a tour of the lockup facility, followed by a tearful personal apology to the owner of the hardware store. I got the message.

With this important caveat, Rabbi Cordovero's instruction is clear: we should open ourselves to assist others with their challenges, even if the challenges are entirely of their own making. In other words, saying "it's not my problem" is in itself the problem. We didn't make the mess, but we should not be above helping to clean it up.

Practical Applications

My first name is Henry, a name that doesn't readily lend itself to the diminutive, but for years an acquaintance insisted on calling me "Hank." People may call me Henry, they may address me with my Hebrew name Hillel, but I will certainly not respond to "Hank." No offense to other Hanks—it's a fine name—but it's not me. I tried without success to dismiss my irritation with this person's use of "Hank." Eventually, I took him aside and politely informed him that I really preferred he stick with "Henry" or "Hillel," but he persisted, even enjoying my consternation. I addressed it again a few weeks later, and he apologized and made a commitment not to continue, but he did so with a slightly patronizing smile, as if the nickname was my problem and not his (probably true, but irrelevant). His disingenuous "repentance" was clearly of the "out of fear" variety, because he wanted to avoided unpleasantness in the future, not because he seriously considered my feelings. Ultimately, I got what I wanted because he stopped saying "Hank," but I never personally really forgave him.

Years later, after having worked on *Date Palm of Devorah* and especially the Third Level of Mercy, I reconsidered my attitude. This person had in fact suffered some serious business losses, and I felt badly for him. Ultimately I realized that I was still carrying around resentment over this minor issue, and it was time to just forget about it all.

Rivka has a favorite coffee mug that figures prominently in her morning routine at the office. Every morning she gets to work, hangs up her jacket, turns on her computer and reaches for her cup to make herself a coffee. One morning, Rivka finds that her mug is not in its usual place at the top right corner of her desk blotter, but she knows where it is anyway—it's sitting in the sink in the office kitchen, stained with Miriam's coral lipstick.

"I don't mind if you use my mug when you work late," Rivka tells Miriam when she shuffles in around eleven, "but would you at least rinse it out and return it to my desk when you're done with it?" Miriam apologizes, and Rivka responds halfheartedly with "it was nothing, don't worry about it," a phrase that barely disguises her profound irritation. By lunchtime, however, Rivka recalls the Third Level of Mercy and resolves to take Miriam's apology seriously, putting some renewed energy into forgiving her.

Spouses in a strong marriage recognize each other's strengths and weaknesses, striving to maximize the former and minimize the latter. I, for example, am completely incompetent in the kitchen, unable to make anything more complicated that spaghetti with margarine (a perennial favorite of the kids, at least till they turned twelve). My wife sometimes comments that as a historian I discovered fascinating, rare materials in formerly secret Soviet archives, but as a husband I can't find anything in the refrigerator. Day in and day out, however, she constantly thinks of my needs and prepares delicious, nutritious meals for the entire family (more on this in Level Six).

The uncontested mistress of the kitchen, I nevertheless discovered a minor and entirely idiosyncratic weakness in her otherwise complete command of everything culinary. Early in our marriage, we were living in a fourth-floor walk-up in the Old Katamon neighborhood. A typical Jerusalem apartment, it featured a glorious view of the sun setting over the gently rolling hills of the city, early-morning wake-ups from the *muezzin* calling Muslims to prayer, and terrazzo floors. The latter were especially unkind to glass, as Ilana discovered late one Friday afternoon as she dropped a large bottle of grape juice. Young and enthusiastic husband that I was, I rushed into the kitchen and immediately set to work cleaning up the broken glass, wiping purple splashes off the cabinets, and concluding with a fresh *sponga* wash while my wife showered and changed. Her gratitude was so overwhelming that this incident ultimately formed the basis of a small family tradition: whenever anything breaks or spills it's my job to clean it up (finally—something I can do right in the kitchen). Obviously, my wife can handle these mishaps, and if I'm not around she does so without complaint. Nevertheless, it's one of the quirks of our marriage that I am the primary spill-and broken-glass cleaner of the family.

I view this as my opportunity to fulfill at least some minor aspect of the Third Level of Mercy. Even though I am not responsible for such occasional mishaps, I happily clean them up, regarding this behavior as a welcome opportunity to express my gratitude and love for Ilana.

The Fourth Level: Remember the Family

Introduction

The Fourth Level of Mercy calls attention to the fundamental connectedness of humanity. The Jewish people in particular maintain a strong familial relationship which Rabbi Cordovero describes as a basic unity, as if each individual Jew constituted a limb of a single body. On a Kabbalistic level, the Jewish people derive their vitality from a single flow of energy, branching out into myriads upon myriads of individuals, but at their root they are essentially one entity, as will be discussed in the commentary below. Rabbi Cordovero's treatment of the well-known Talmudic teaching (Sanhedrin 27b) that "all Jews are responsible for each other" may be understood in its literal sense: "all Jews are tied (ערב) to one another." *Date Palm of Devorah* explores the meaning of this concept in the context of the creation of a minyan, or prayer quorum.

This familial connection carries two implications that are especially relevant to the concept of Forgiveness. First, Rabbi Cordovero borrows a human metaphor to reveal the Kabbalistic secret of the suffering of the Divine Parent: just as a mother or father experiences pain when a child is anguished, so too does God suffer over our tribulations, so to speak. Second, Rabbi Cordovero extends the metaphor to the requisite behavior of siblings, who must carry greater levels of tolerance for each other than they would for strangers. This latter point brings his treatment of the Fourth Level to a conclusion with a discussion of the special level of forgiveness that Jews, as a family, must have for each other. The principles of this Level may be applied beyond the Jewish people as a whole, but Rabbi

Cordovero directs his attention here to a specific audience.

הרביעית - לִשְׁאֵרִית נַחֲלָתוֹ

הִנֵּה הב"ה מִתְנַהֵג עִם יִשְׂרָאֵל בְּדֶרֶךְ זוֹ אוֹמַר מַה אֶעֱשֶׂה לְיִשְׂרָאֵל וְהֵם קְרוֹבַי שְׁאֵר בָּשָׂר יֵשׁ לִי עִמָּהֶם שֶׁהֵם בַּת זוּג לְהב"ה וְקוֹרֵא לָהּ בִּתִּי, אֲחוֹתִי, אִמִּי. כְּדְפֵרְשׁוּ ז"ל וּכְתִיב יִשְׂרָאֵל עַם קְרוֹבוֹ מַמָּשׁ קָרֳבָה יֵשׁ לוֹ עִמָּהֶם וּבָנָיו הֵם.

וְהַיְנוּ לִשְׁאֵרִית נַחֲלָתוֹ לָשׁוֹן שְׁאֵר בָּשָׂר וְסוֹף סוֹף הֵם נַחֲלָתוֹ. וּמַה אָמַר, אִם אֲעַנִּישֵׁם הֲרֵי הַכְּאֵב עָלַי כְּדִכְתִיב בְּכָל צָרָתָם לֹא צָר.

כְּתִיב בְּ'אָלֶף' לוֹמַר שֶׁצַּעֲרָם מַגִּיעַ לְפֶלֶא הָעֶלְיוֹן וְכָל שֶׁכֵּן לְדוּ פַּרְצוּפִין שֶׁבָּהֶן עִיקָר הַהַנְהָגָה דְקָרֵינוּ בְּ'וָאו' לוֹ צָר.

וּכְתִיב וַתִּקְצַר נַפְשׁוֹ בַּעֲמַל יִשְׂרָאֵל לְפִיכָךְ אֵינוֹ סוֹבֵל צַעֲרָם וְלֹא קְלוֹנָם מִפְּנֵי שֶׁהֵם שְׁאֵרִית נַחֲלָתוֹ.

כָּךְ הָאָדָם עִם חֲבֵרוֹ כָּל יִשְׂרָאֵל הֵם שְׁאֵר בָּשָׂר אֵלּוּ עִם אֵלּוּ מִפְּנֵי שֶׁהַנְּשָׁמוֹת כְּלוּלוֹת יַחַד יֵשׁ בָּזֶה חֵלֶק זֶה וּבָזֶה חֵלֶק זֶה, וּלְכָךְ אֵינוֹ דוֹמֶה מְרֻבִּים

הָעוֹשִׂים אֶת הַמִּצְוֹת וְכוּ' מִפְּנֵי כְּלָלוּתָם, וּלְכָךְ פֵּרְשׁוּ רַבּוֹתֵינוּ זִכְרוֹנָם לִבְרָכָה עַל הַגְּמָרָא מֵעֲשָׂרָה רִאשׁוֹנִים בְּבֵית הַכְּנֶסֶת אֲפִלּוּ מֵאָה בָּאִים אַחֲרָיו מְקַבֵּל שָׂכָר כְּנֶגֶד כֻּלָּם, מֵאָה מַמָּשׁ כְּמַשְׁמָעוֹ, מִפְּנֵי שֶׁהָעֲשָׂרָה הֵם כְּלוּלִים אֵלּוּ בְּאֵלּוּ הֲרֵי הֵם עֲשָׂרָה פְּעָמִים עֲשָׂרָה מֵאָה וְכָל אֶחָד מֵהֶם כָּלוּל מִמֵּאָה אִם כֵּן אֲפִלּוּ יָבוֹאוּ מֵאָה הוּא יֵשׁ לוֹ שָׂכָר מֵאָה, וְכֵן מִטַּעַם זֶה יִשְׂרָאֵל עֲרֵבִים זֶה לָזֶה מִפְּנֵי שֶׁמַּמָּשׁ יֵשׁ בְּכָל אֶחָד חֵלֶק אַחֵר מֵחֲבֵרוֹ וּכְשֶׁחוֹטֵא הָאֶחָד פּוֹגֵם אֶת עַצְמוֹ וּפוֹגֵם חֵלֶק אֲשֶׁר לַחֲבֵרוֹ בּוֹ, נִמְצָא מִצַּד הַחֵלֶק הַהוּא חֲבֵרוֹ עָרֵב עָלָיו. אִם כֵּן הֵם שֶׁאָר זֶה עִם זֶה

לְכָךְ רָאוּי לְאָדָם לִהְיוֹתוֹ חָפֵץ בְּטוֹבָתוֹ שֶׁל חֲבֵירוֹ וְעֵינוֹ טוֹבָה עַל טוֹבַת חֲבֵרוֹ וּכְבוֹדוֹ יִהְיֶה חָבִיב עָלָיו כְּשֶׁלּוֹ שֶׁהֲרֵי הוּא הוּא מַמָּשׁ, וּמִטַּעַם זֶה נִצְטַוֵּינוּ וְאָהַבְתָּ לְרֵעֲךָ כָּמוֹךָ.

וְרָאוּי שֶׁיִּרְצֶה בְּכַשְׁרוּת חֲבֵרוֹ וְלֹא יְדַבֵּר בִּגְנוּתוֹ כְּלָל וְלֹא יִרְצֶה בּוֹ כְּדֶרֶךְ שֶׁאֵין הב"ה רוֹצֶה בִּגְנוּתֵנוּ וְלֹא בְּצַעֲרֵנוּ מִטַּעַם הַקִּרְבָה, אַף הוּא לֹא יִרְצֶה בִּגְנוּת חֲבֵרוֹ וְלֹא בְּצַעֲרוֹ וְלֹא בְּקִלְקוּלוֹ וְיֵרַע לוֹ מִמֶּנּוּ כְּאִלּוּ הוּא מַמָּשׁ הָיָה שָׁרוּי בְּאוֹתוֹ צַעַר אוֹ בְּאוֹתוֹ טוֹבָה:

The Fourth Level

For the Remnant of His Inheritance

Behold, God treats the Jewish people in this manner, saying "what shall I do with Israel, for they are my family, I share one flesh with them?" They are the marriage partner of God, who calls them "my daughter, my sister, my mother." This is as the Rabbis explained, and as it is written: *Israel, the nation related to God*, literally related to God. They are God's children.

This is the meaning of *the remnant of His inheritance*, a phrase that implies a familial relationship, and in end they are His inheritance. What does God say? "If I punish them, behold it pains me," as it is written: *with all their pain—it is painful to Him*.

The word *to Him* [לו] is written with an *alef* [לא] as if to say that their pain reaches the highest mystery, and how much more so the "two faces," which are essential to direction. Nevertheless we pronounce this word as if it were written with a *vav*, meaning *it is painful to Him*.

This is as it is written: *and His soul was grieved by the anguish of Israel*, because God does not tolerate their pain and insult, since they are the remnant of His inheritance.

So too should a person treat another. All Israel are related to each other, for their souls are all bound as one—each Jew has a portion of the other's soul and vice versa. In this manner, "one cannot compare the act of many people performing a commandment [to one person acting alone]" because they are gathered together. This is what the Sages said regarding the first ten people who create a prayer quorum in the synagogue: even if a hundred people enter afterward, the first ten receive merit equivalent to them all, literally the merit of the hundred latecomers. This is because the first ten is contained within the hundred, which is ten times ten, a hundred. Each one of them is contained within the hundred, and if so, even if a hundred come, each of the first ten has the merit of the hundred. Also for this reason, all Jews are responsible for one another, because each of them literally possesses a portion of each other. When one of them sins, he harms himself as well as harming the portion of himself that resides in the other, since he is connected to his part that is contained within his fellow. They are related to each other.

Thus it is appropriate for a person to seek the benefit of one's fellow, showing him a generosity of spirit. He should consider his dignity as dear to him as his own, for they are literally a single entity. Because of this we are commanded, "and you will love your fellow as yourself."

It is fitting that a person support the fundamental goodness of another and not speak evil of him at all. One should not wish for anything that is inconsistent with what God desires for that person, neither his disgrace nor his suffering, for they are related to God. A person should not wish to see another's downfall, nor suffering, nor any harm at all, and view the situation of as if he himself were immersed in the same suffering, or exalting in the same good fortune.

Commentary

The Jewish people have a distinct role in the Divine plan, and as such the Bible refers to them as *am segulah* (Exodus 19:5) or "cherished people." Evident in much Rabbinic literature and prominent in Kabbalistic thought, the concept of *am segulah* may be taken as an expression of ethnocentrism, but is more properly understood as the expression of the Jews' sense of destiny and responsibility to the world as a whole. Scattered across the globe in the aftermath of an ancient exile, the Jewish people nevertheless maintained faith with their God, committed to their mission serving as the "light unto the nations" (Isaiah 45:6).

Whether they are conscious of this responsibility or not, all Jews are united in this single purpose, and each individual Jew is crucial to the unfolding of the Divine Plan. Elsewhere in his writings (*Pardes Rimonim* 2:78a, cited in Rabbi Gavra's commentary), Rabbi Cordovero provides a beautiful image to illustrate the relationship of the individual to the whole. Imagine, he writes, a beautiful spring of fresh water, running clear and strong from a source that is as wide as a beam. That spring is fed by thousands upon thousands of smaller springs that originate in the deep, each one of them no wider than the diameter of a needle, yet come together to make this impressive, constant artesian well. If one of those tiny springs were to be clogged up, the overall flow of the large spring would be ineluctably reduced by that same amount, and the other miniature springs would not be able to replace the missing water.

So too, continues Rabbi Cordovero, with the Jewish people as a whole. Each individual contributes a small amount of flow of positive energy into the Universe, greater or lesser, but they all combine to generate a massive, single conduit of holiness as part of their divine mission in the world. Should the flow from even one of those Jews decrease as a result of transgression or other wrongdoing, the overarching purpose of the entire people is delayed. Jews must remain conscious of their interrelationship and shared task. Thus it is every Jew's responsibility to help his or her fellow return to a state of maximum capacity, repairing the sin and restoring the flow of positive energy to the world.

Bound together by this awesome task, Rabbi Cordovero uses several powerful metaphors to represent the Jews and their relationship with God, each alluding to Biblical verses: bride, beloved, daughter, mother. Rabbi Landau expands on the differences between these terms: "My bride" refers to the relationship in its newness, fresh with promise; "My beloved" encompasses the notion of partnership, of shared goals; "My daughter," the unique love of a parent for a child; "My sister," self-sacrifice for the other; "My mother," a love that combines both honor and respect.

The love of a parent receives additional attention, in the specific context of shared pain. A loving parent cannot issue punishment without sharing in the pain of the child. *Date Palm of Devorah* demonstrates the notion of Divine "pain" through an unusual Biblical phenomenon, the distinction between the *keri* and the *ketiv* of a word. The *keri* refers to the way a word is *pronounced*, whereas the *ketiv* refers to the way the word is *spelled*. The Hebrew language contains numerous homonyms, or words that are pronounced identically yet have very different meanings (consider the English words "led" as in 'he led me to the store' and the metal "lead"). In Biblical homonyms, the principal meaning is generally derived from the *keri* (pronunciation) rather than the *ketiv* (written form). The homonym in the verse cited by Rabbi Cordovero (Isaiah 63:9) is *spelled* "in all their pain, He has no pain," but the accepted *meaning* is "in all their pain, He *has* pain," exactly the opposite. According to the *ketiv*, God is unmoved by human suffering, perhaps an allusion to the transcendental divide that separates finite humans and the infinite Being. According to the *keri*, however, the accepted meaning of the verse is the opposite: when the Jews suffer, God also suffers.

Human suffering reaches to the "highest mystery," a term used to describe the *sefirah* of Keter, the source comes all mercy (the letters in the Hebrew word "mystery," or *pele*, may be reversed to spell *alef*, a reference to the first *sefirah*). The suffering certainly affects the sixth and tenth *sefirot* (Tiferet and Malkhut, respectively), which are placed directly below Keter. According to Kabbalistic metaphysics, Tiferet and Malkhut, known as the "two faces" (*du partsufim*) are the principal *sefirot* through which God affects the world. Tiferet represents the culmination and balancing of the flow of Divine energy, and Malkhut represents the reception of this energy in the world as we perceive it. *Date Palm of Devorah* thus indicates that the suffering of the Jews has an impact on the volume and direction of the current of vitality that flows from the Divine Parent to the universe as a whole. Imagine, for example, if a child is hospitalized, God forbid, and her parent has to leave her bedside to go to work. Distraught and distracted, the parent's performance at work will certainly suffer until the child is restored to health. Similarly, argues Rabbi Cordovero, the suffering of the Jews has a negative influence on the way in which God conducts the business of the world. In the words of Judges 10:16, God is *grieved by the anguish of Israel*. The doctrine that God somehow feels the pain of the Jewish people because they share a special, familial relationship does not exempt from punishment, as Rabbi Shaynberg explains. The Jewish people are singled out for a unique mission, and if anything the mission assures that they have a greater exposure to Divine punishment given the importance of the task.

Besides the mission-based special relationship between God and the Jewish people, all Jews are in a special relationship with each other because they quite literally share the same soul. According to the Kabbalah, there are five levels to the human soul, three of which are located in the human body and two of which remain in a Heavenly source. Beginning from lowest to highest, the *nefesh* is the most basic animating force, and is associated in particular with blood and the liver; the *ruah* finds its locus in the heart, and the *neshamah* in the brain. These are not so much distinct units as different levels of the same vital energy, like liquid in a bottle—the heaviest elements of the liquid, including the sediment, sinks to the bottom, the middle of the bottle contains the liquid with heavier elements in suspension, and the top level contains the purest form of the liquid. The source of this soul-liquid is a massive, two-tiered vat with individual spigots directing the flow into each human being: *hayah* is the name of the lower level of this vat, and *yehidah* the higher.

Every Jew possesses a specific *nefesh, ruah* and *neshamah* (abbreviated NaRaN) but all Jews derive their individual NaRaN from the same source: *hayah* and *yehidah*. Moreover, this is a dynamic system: the NaRaN is continually connected to the *hayah* and *yehidah*, receiving more soul-material at every moment, like a vat that constantly pours out wine, or perhaps like a generator that ceaselessly provides electricity. Thus all Jews, sharing *hayah* and *yehidah*, literally share the same soul, bound together at the highest level of existence.

Rabbi Cordovero illustrates the power of the collective identity of the Jewish people with a Midrashic teaching (*Sifra*, Behukotai 1:4) regarding the formation of a *minyan*, or prayer quorum. If less than ten worshippers are present, there is no *minyan*, and the Torah may not be read with its traditional blessings, but once ten are present, the *minyan* is complete and all prayers may be recited. Even if a hundred worshippers eventually gather for prayer, they do not alter the fundamental status of the quorum that was created by the first ten. The reason for this, explains Rabbi Epstein in his phenomenal commentary on *Date Palm of Devorah*, is that the first ten worshippers correspond to the ten *sefirot*, which together make up the human image of God known as the Supernal Adam. Once complete, the Supernal Adam cannot become more complete. Rabbi Epstein compares this to the opening of a door to a darkened hall: each person who enters opens the door wider, allowing more sunlight into the room. Once the door is open to its furthest extent, many more people may enter, but the flow of sunlight is already fully optimized.

Returning to the theme of forgiveness, Rabbi Cordovero reveals the imperative contained in the Fourth Level of Mercy: since all Jews are connected to each other, they have an enhanced responsibility to show each other kindness, being of one family and one fate. Rabbi Epstein cites a memorable teaching of the 20th century Rabbi Eliyahu Dessler, based on a parable in the Jerusalem Talmud (*Nedarim* 9:4): A man is cutting meat, and the knife accidentally cuts his hand. Does he even imagine for a moment that the left hand should take revenge on the right hand for the injury? Not at all, that would be absurd! And yet the Jewish people are no less related to each other than one hand is to the other. The pain felt by one Jew is shared by all others, as they are united in a single soul. Rabbi Shaynberg illustrates this with a powerful citation from the Midrash (*Mekhilta*, Yitro, also *Vayikra Rabah* 84:6): "Why are the Jewish people compared to a sheep? When a sheep is struck on one of its limbs, its entire body feels it the pain. So the Jewish people: when one of them sins, they all feel the consequences. Rabbi Shimon ben Yohai taught: this is like two men who are sailing on a boat. One of them takes an axe and begins to chop a hole in the hull. The other man exclaims, 'what are you doing!?' and the first man responds, 'why should you care? Am I not chopping under my own seat?'" The Jew may think he is only damaging his own spot in the boat, but in reality the entire ship is placed in danger by his actions.

We will return to this metaphor in Part II of this work, because in many ways it mirrors Cordoveran Kabbalah as a whole. The flow of positive human energy not only benefits the world through its immediate effect, it also arouses the Divine *Sefirot* to act in kind, sending a much larger flow of similarly charged positive energy into the Universe. In this manner, the recognition of our responsibilities for the welfare of others is a mandate that bears cosmic implications. In the context of the Fourth Level of Mercy, the teaching of Rabbi Cordovero's illustrious student is especially relevant. Rabbi Isaac Luria (the Arizal) famously instructed his followers to precede the morning prayers with a firm dedication to observe the commandment to "love your fellow as yourself" (Leviticus 19:18). Recognizing the fundamental connectedness of humanity, we open wide the door to the darkened hall.

Practical Applications

"Didn't you wear that at the Cohen bar mitzvah last year?" Tzippora's tone is innocent, but Shayna gets what she is really saying—her wardrobe is getting tired, and everyone knows it. After all, here it is several months later and she's wearing the same dress at another bar mitzvah. Shayna manages to smile, seething with anger and resentment, but before she can respond, someone bumps into Tzippora's elbow and she spills red wine all over her new cream-colored outfit.

The German language has the perfect term to describe the emotion Shayna feels: *Schadenfreude,* or "joy at the downfall of another." After a moment, though, Shayna recalls the *Date Palm of Devorah* and forces herself to recognize that she and Tzippora are actually sisters, related to each other as all Jews, sharing a single soul. She rebukes herself for quietly rejoicing over the messy accident by placing herself in Tzippora's position and imagining how she feels. Shayna blunts her secret satisfaction with a bit of shared pain.

Harold realizes he spends far too much time and energy gossiping. He consults with his Rabbi, who instructs him to engage in daily study of Rabbi Israel Meir Kagan's classic work, *Hafets Hayim* (*Chofetz Chaim*), a brilliant work that codifies the Jewish perspective on the dignity of human speech. Harold learns that, according to Jewish law, the dissemination of negative information about an individual is completely prohibited—even if the story is completely true! Shocked and chastened, Harold reads further to learn that while his gossip is totally forbidden, nevertheless there are situations where the revealing of a derogatory report may be warranted. The only way Harold can share such stories is if it meets a stringent test consisting of seven criteria: the rule of SILENCE, an acronym for all seven preconditions:

Search for details that may exonerate the individual from wrongdoing. Harold has to make sure that the subject of the negative information really deserves to be accused of this inappropriate activity, and that it is fair to lay this charge at his or her feet.

Intend a positive, practical result. Under no circumstances should the negative information be circulated for purposes of entertainment. The only possible reason to reveal anyone's faults is to prevent harm in the future, or redress a wrong that requires resolution.

Look for alternatives to revealing the negative information. Perhaps the positive, practical result could be achieved by means other than revealing the negative information?

Exaggeration is forbidden. If the negative information must be revealed, it is important that it remain completely factual, uncolored by editorial comment or bias.

No hearsay is allowed. Harold must have direct, personal knowledge of the facts, and not rely on the reports of others.

Consequences of revealing the information must be proportionate. Sometimes a minor indiscretion may have such colossal implications that, even though the wrong is addressed, a far greater damage is imposed on another person. Is this something that should simply be ignored?

Engage the subject first. If all the conditions are met and the negative information may be revealed, Harold has to talk to the person involved and give him or her a chance to rectify the situation on his or her own.

These laws are complex and deserve more attention that can be devoted in the scope of this brief work. Harold recognizes this, and commits himself to upholding the Fourth Level of Mercy by undertaking regular review of the laws prohibiting gossip.

The Fifth Level: Release the Anger

Introduction

The prophet Zechariah portrays God as a shepherd with two staffs: one is called "pleasantness" (נעם) and the other is called "woundings" (חובלים). In his commentary on *Date Palm of Devorah*, Rabbi Epstein explains the simile: just as a shepherd may choose to lead some sheep with gentle prodding, using the staff of pleasantness, he may also direct his flock by striking them aggressively, using the staff of woundings. So too, God may elect to lead us by opening doors of opportunity and allowing us to advance on our own, or God may choose to force us to follow a path against our will, using harsh penalties. Either way, as Rabbi Cordovero puts it, "God behaves with hardness or with softness, all for the benefit of the Jewish people."

In the Fifth Level of Mercy, Rabbi Cordovero explains that God will use the staff of pleasantness even if a person is undeserving. Borrowing from an episode in Jewish history recorded in II Kings, Rabbi Cordovero proves that God expanded the boundaries of ancient Israel under King Jeroboam even though the people did not repent. Counterintuitively, God may choose to use the staff of pleasantness if it is clear that the staff of woundings will not achieve the desired results.

Applied to the human level, Date Palm of Devorah urges us to consider switching tactics when dealing with difficult people. Sometimes an act of unmitigated forgiveness is required, even though the circumstances seem to demand retaliation or retribution.

החמישית - לֹא הֶחֱזִיק לָעַד אַפּוֹ

זוֹ מִדָּה אַחֶרֶת שֶׁאֲפִלּוּ שֶׁהָאָדָם מַחֲזִיק בְּחֵטְא אֵין הב"ה מַחֲזִיק אַף, וְאִם יַחֲזִיק לֹא לָעַד אֶלָּא יְבַטֵּל כַּעֲסוֹ אֲפִלּוּ שֶׁלֹּא יָשׁוּב הָאָדָם.

כְּמוֹ שֶׁמָּצִינוּ בִּימֵי יָרָבְעָם בֶּן יוֹאָשׁ שֶׁהֶחֱזִיר הב"ה גְּבוּל יִשְׂרָאֵל וְהֵם הָיוּ עוֹבְדִים עֲגָלִים וְרִחֵם עֲלֵיהֶם וְלֹא שָׁבוּ.

אִם כֵּן לָמָּה רִחֵם, בִּשְׁבִיל מִדָּה זוֹ שֶׁלֹּא הֶחֱזִיק לָעַד אַפּוֹ אַדְּרַבָּא מַחֲלִישׁ אַפּוֹ עִם הֱיוֹת שֶׁעֲדַיִן הַחֵטְא קַיָּם אֵינוֹ מַעֲנִישׁ אֶלָּא מְצַפֶּה וּמְרַחֵם אוּלַי יָשׁוּבוּ, וְהַיְנוּ כִּי לֹא לָנֶצַח אָרִיב וְלֹא לְעוֹלָם אֶטּוֹר.

אֶלָּא הב"ה מִתְנַהֵג בְּרַכּוּת וּבְבַקָּשׁוֹת הַכֹּל לְטוֹבַת יִשְׂרָאֵל

וְזוֹ מִדָּה רְאוּיָה לָאָדָם לְהִתְנַהֵג בָּהּ אִם חֲבֵרוֹ אֲפִלּוּ שֶׁהוּא רַשַּׁאי לְהוֹכִיחַ בְּיִסּוּרִים אֶת חֲבֵרוֹ אוֹ אֶת בָּנָיו וְהֵם מִתְיַסְּרִים לֹא מִפְּנֵי זֶה יַרְבֶּה תּוֹכַחְתּוֹ וְלֹא יַחֲזִיק כַּעֲסוֹ אֲפִלּוּ שֶׁכָּעַס אֶלָּא יְבַטְּלֶנּוּ וְלֹא יַחֲזִיק לָעַד אַפּוֹ.

גַּם אִם הוּא אַף הַמֻּתָּר לָאָדָם כְּעֵין שֶׁפֵּרְשׁוּ כִּי תִרְאֶה חֲמוֹר שֹׂנַאֲךָ וְגוֹ' וּפֵרְשׁוּ מַהוּ הַשִּׂנְאָה הַזֹּאת שֶׁרָאָה אוֹתוֹ עוֹבֵר עֲבֵרָה וְהוּא יָחִיד אֵינוּ יָכוֹל לְהָעִיד וְשֹׂנֵא אוֹתוֹ עַל דָּבָר וַאֲפִלּוּ הָכִי אָמְרָה תּוֹרָה עָזֹב תַּעֲזֹב עִמּוֹ שְׁבוֹק יָת דְּבְלִבָּךְ אֶלָּא מִצְוָה לְקָרֵב אוֹתוֹ בְּאַהֲבָה אוּלַי יוֹעִיל בְּדֶרֶךְ זֶה וְהַיְנוּ מַמָּשׁ מִדָּה זוֹ לֹא הֶחֱזִיק לָעַד אַפּוֹ:

The Fifth Level

He Does Not Hold Fast to His Anger Forever

This is another Level. Even when a person holds fast to a negative behavior pattern, God does not hold fast to His anger, and even if God does hold fast, it is only temporary. Rather, God nullifies His wrath even if the person does not repent.

This is as we find with Jeroboam son of Joash, for whom God restored the boundaries of Israel, even though they were worshipping idols. God had mercy on them even when they did not return.

If this is so, why did God have mercy? It was because of this Level: God does not hold fast to His anger forever. On the contrary, God actively weakens His own anger, such that even when the sin persists, God does not punish. God waits and extends mercy—perhaps they will repent! This is the meaning of *not forever will He fight, and not forever will He exact retribution.*

God behaves with softness and with

hardness, all for the benefit of the Jewish people.

This is an appropriate Level for people to use with one another. Even if one would have the right to rebuke or punish another, or rebuke or punish children, and they would be required to accept the suffering, this does not mean that the person should exercise that right excessively. A person should not hold fast to anger, even when it is deeply felt. Rather, a person should nullify it and not hold fast to this anger.

Even if this anger would be permitted, as the Rabbis understand the verse, *when you see the donkey of the one you hate lying under its burden*, and they explain, "What kind of hatred is this? When a person is a lone witness to another's transgression, the testimony is invalid, and therefore he hates him for his act." Nevertheless the Torah teaches, *you shall surely help the other*. Abandon what is in your heart! It is a commandment to draw that person close with love, and perhaps this approach will help. This is literally the Level under discussion: *He does not hold fast to His anger forever.*

Commentary

Anger is a habit. There are certain people, certain times, certain issues, that seem to be especially likely to produce anger, and often with good reason. How many times was that child asked to clean his room? How often does a spouse have to be reminded to pick up the dry cleaning? Anger often follows a pattern as easy to predict as the path of the sun on a cloudless day, and it's no surprise that we "hold fast" to that anger, ready to engage it at a moment's notice once the various elements fall into place in their expected fashion.

God, however, is not subject to the laws of habit. Furthermore, no one can deny that when God is angered (whatever that anthropomorphism really means), we humans are deserving, since we have certainly received clear instructions and understand the consequences for non-compliance. Nevertheless, when God sees that humans are once again following inappropriate patterns of behavior (worshipping golden calves, for example), God does not immediately engage Divine anger and allow it to reverberate throughout the fragile Universe. Rather, God actively engages his anger with a message of forgiveness, extending tolerance to humanity even when they are undeserving. With full consciousness that humanity was expected to do better, God nevertheless extends an additional measure of forgiveness, repaying ingratitude with kindness, as we see with the military victories of King Jeroboam even at a time when the Jewish people engaged in idolatry.

Rabbi Cordovero cites a passage from Psalms (103:9) to illustrate this attribute: *not forever will God fight*, and many of the commentators provide an additional passage, cited in the daily liturgy (Habakuk 3:2): *in anger, You remember mercy*. The Fifth Level of Mercy is God's ability to remember mercy at a time of anger. Human beings, by way of contrast, do precisely the opposite—in anger, we forget mercy. God remembers, while we forget.

Our task is to recognize that we experience anger like the sudden, uncontrolled acceleration of a car. Angered by the slow driver ahead of us, we tense up, our blood pressure rises, and we shoot forward into the passing lane, shortening our potential response time to obstacles and increasing the potential of an accident. Obviously, the right thing to do under such a circumstance is to reconsider carefully our driving options—for example, we may have a right turn coming up at the next block which would require us to move dangerously back into the right lane, cutting off another driver. The urge to surge is immediate, and even though the most rational course of action might be to simply ease up on the gas pedal, this is easier said than done: anger is an emotion that swallows a person whole, leaving little room for reconsideration and reflection. The right foot seems to have a mind of its own, and the velocity seems inescapable.

The Fifth Level points out another strategy: if you have difficulty removing your right foot from the gas pedal, then pick up your left foot and apply pressure to the brake pedal. Your right foot may be adding the volatile fuel-air mixture to the engine, and you will hear it roaring in complaint, but it will have to work harder to overcome the resistance of the brakes. This is not ideal driving technique, but the investment of energy in actively decelerating the vehicle may prevent disaster.

The Fifth Level makes two simultaneous demands: on the one hand, it argues that a person has the right to maintain expectations of proper standards from others, hoping for their improvement and working to shape their behavior. On the other hand, the Fifth Level pleads for the difficulty of change, and begs a person to extend a grace period for the transgressions of others. The key element here is that a person must find new strategies to deal with the unproductive emotion of anger, freeing up energy to help the offending individual reform his or her behavior. Simply pushing back against the incorrect behavior is both insufficient and counterproductive.

Here's a metaphor that will be well-understood by those who live close to a coastline. The ocean sometimes produces dangerous currents called "rip tides" or "rip currents." An unwary swimmer may become caught in one of these powerful rip currents, and find him- or herself suddenly pulled tens, even hundreds of yards out to sea. Escaping these currents is not difficult, but it requires an active strategy: one may not take the obvious route of swimming back to shore, because the current is simply too strong and the swimmer will become exhausted with the effort, exposed to greater danger as the current surges further out into the open ocean. Rather, one must swim *perpendicular* to the current, following the coastline rather than heading towards it. Even though this means a partial surrender to the rip current, by taking this strategy a swimmer will shortly escape the current, and then be able to swim back to the safety of dry land.

Rabbi Cordovero argues that this technique must be used for anger as well. When irritated, reacting against the cause of the complaint may actually escalate the crisis, making the possibility of a peaceful reconciliation more distant. In other words, reacting with anger is like attempting to swim against the rip current. The Fifth Level demands another approach, requiring a fresh infusion of energy directly into *forgiving* the offender, as counterintuitive as swimming perpendicular to the shore.

This technique is very useful when one is the object of someone else's anger, and especially if the accusation is baseless or exaggerated (a recipe for interpersonal disaster if there ever was one). If the worst response is countering this anger with anger, the second worst is telling the person who is angry to simply "calm down" (two words that, in my humble opinion, should be removed from the working vocabulary of any marriage). The Fifth Level might be invoked at this point, and a person might consider internally saying "I certainly don't deserve this treatment, and I would be within my rights to rebuke this person for accusing me, but I'm going to dig deep and see if I can find a reserve of respect and even affection for this person, and allow their anger to simply wash over me and exhaust itself in the process. Once this person calms down —it may take a while—then I can address the cause of this anger, and perhaps even indicate how unfairly I was treated." Achieving this level of awareness is truly an illustration of the passage from Habakuk: *in anger, You remember mercy.*

Rabbi Cordovero concludes his discussion of the Fifth Level with a complex image from the Torah about a man who sees that his enemy's donkey has collapsed under its poorly distributed burden (Exodus 23:5, discussed at length in the Talmud, *Pesahim* 103b). The Torah forbids cruelty to animals, and thus the man is obligated to release the burden from the donkey's back and allow it to stand. The Torah goes even further, and obligates him to help his enemy reload the donkey properly by stating *you shall certainly help him.*

The Hebrew word for "help" (עזב), in other contexts, may mean "abandon," its diametric opposite. Which meaning is intended here? Rabbi Cordovero resolves the ambiguity with a quotation from the ancient Aramaic translation of Onkelos, who renders *you shall certainly help him* as "abandon that which is in your heart." Onkelos' reading is that the man should help his enemy by abandoning the hatred he has for him in his heart. Even if his hatred is based on fact, even if he personally saw him committing a transgression but is unable to testify against him in court, nevertheless he must abandon the hatred in his heart and get to the task of helping his erstwhile enemy.

If the Torah requires us to take this approach with our enemies, how much more so would we be required to do so with those we love.

Practical Applications

The warning light went on as Shlomo and Shayna are pulling out of the garage. Shlomo turns to Shayna and says, "Why didn't you just gas up when it dropped to the quarter-tank?" There's more than a note of irritation in his voice, and Shayna knows how unfair it all is—one of the kids took the car out last night, and it was well above a quarter-tank when he left. She could respond with some cutting remark about Shlomo's poor memory, because after all he was the one who gave the keys to their son. Shayna has been reading *Date Palm of Devorah*, however, so she decides to take a deep, cleansing breath and not respond in kind. She thinks about the stress he's under at work, and she takes a soft tone of voice when she says, "we should have given him some money to put gas in the tank," completely ignoring his unfair accusation.

Shlomo, however, is not as assiduous a student as his wife. When they get home, he's ready to have it out with their teenage son Sidney.

"What's wrong with you," Shlomo says as he warms up to his regular rant. "Can't you ever think about others? Why are you so selfish? Couldn't you at least let us know that the tank was almost empty? We were late because of you!" Sidney glares dully at his father which reminds Shlomo of a series of Sidney's irritating teenage behaviors. Shlomo's internal temperature rises, and he is about to launch into a truly memorable speech that will once and for all cure his son of his immaturity, when he recalls the Fifth Level of Mercy: he has given this speech several times in the last month alone, without a meaningful response from Sidney. Shlomo decides to put away the stick of woundings and take out the stick of pleasantness—precisely *because* Sidney is undeserving, having demonstrated that he will not change as a result of earlier punishments—so Shlomo decides to swim perpendicular to the rip current of his anger.

"I don't think I told you how pleased I was with your grade on that Math midterm," says Shlomo as he sits on the sofa beside him. "Here's a twenty as a reward, treat yourself to something nice." Surprised by this sudden act of kindness, Sidney even takes out one earbud to make sure he heard correctly. Sidney takes the proffered cash and says, "uh, thanks, Dad. Listen, I meant to tell you that the fuel light went on last night, and you should probably put some gas in the car."

The Sixth Level: Who Makes Your Lunch?

Introduction

The Sixth Level begins with a deeply mystical passage in Ezekiel, set in the years immediately prior to the destruction of the first Temple in the sixth century before the common era. God is angered by the sins of the Jewish people, and sends the archangel Gabriel to destroy them utterly, once and for all. Gabriel takes the glowing coals from a space called the *galgal*, located beneath the altar, and prepares to shower devastation upon the people. Gabriel is delayed in place for six years until the image of a human hand appears in the *galgal*, a symbolic representation of the acts of human kindness that the otherwise sinful Jews do for each other. With the appearance of this hand, God cancels Gabriel's mission.

God's mindful delay to act from anger for six years, followed by a recollection of an unrelated kind deed that ultimately averts punishment, is the expression of the Sixth Level of Mercy: for He desires kindness.

Rabbi Cordovero goes on to describe how this Level may be applied on a human scale, offering an exceptionally practical suggestion to promote forgiveness. When angered or frustrated by the behavior of another, one should focus on a single redeeming characteristic or activity of that person. This small technique places a momentary deterrent in the path of reaction through anger, allowing forgiveness to take hold and ultimately blunt the full force of one's wrath.

השישית - כִּי חָפֵץ חֶסֶד הוּא

כְּבָר פֵּרַשְׁנוּ בִּמְקוֹמוֹ שֶׁיֵּשׁ בַּהֵיכָל יָדוּעַ מַלְאָכִים מְמֻנִּים לְקַבֵּל גְּמִילוּת חֶסֶד שֶׁבְּנֵי אדם עוֹשִׂים בָּעוֹלָם הַזֶּה, וְכַאֲשֶׁר מִדַּת הַדִּין מְקַטְרֶגֶת עַל יִשְׂרָאֵל, מִיָּד אוֹתָם הַמַּלְאָכִים מַרְאִים הַחֶסֶד הַהוּא וְהַב"ה מְרַחֵם עַל יִשְׂרָאֵל מִפְּנֵי שֶׁהוּא חָפֵץ בְּחֶסֶד, וְעִם הֱיוֹת שֶׁהֵם חַיָּבִים אִם הֵם גּוֹמְלִים חֶסֶד זֶה לָזֶה מְרַחֵם עֲלֵיהֶם, וּכְמוֹ שֶׁהָיָה בִּזְמַן הַחֻרְבָּן שֶׁנֶּאֱמַר לְגַבְרִיאֵל בֹּא אֶל בֵּינוֹת לַגַּלְגַּל וְגוֹ' פֵּ' דהיינו גבריאל שלקח גחלים להשליך על ישראל והיינו סוד גבריאל שַׂר הַדִּין וְהַגְּבוּרָה וְנָתַן לוֹ רְשׁוּת לְקַבֵּל כֹּחוֹת הַדִּין בֵּינוֹת לַגַּלְגַּל מִתַּחַת לַכְּרוּבִים מֵאֵשׁ הַמִּזְבֵּחַ דְּהַיְנוּ דִּין גְּבוּרַת הַמַּלְכוּת וְהָיָה הַדִּין מִתְחַזֵּק עַד שֶׁבִּקֵּשׁ לְכַלּוֹת אֶת הַכֹּל לְקַעְקֵעַ בֵּיצָתָן שֶׁל יִשְׂרָאֵל מִפְּנֵי שֶׁנִּתְחַיְּבוּ כְּלָיָה וּכְתִיב וַיֵּרָא לַכְּרוּבִים תַּבְנִית יַד אָדָם תַּחַת כַּנְפֵיהֶם וְהַיְנוּ שֶׁאָמַר הב"ה גַבְרִיאֵל הֵם גּוֹמְלִים חֲסָדִים אֵלּוּ עִם אֵלּוּ וְאַף אִם הֵם חַיָּבִים נִצּוֹלוּ וְהָיָה לָהֶם שְׁאֵרִית. וְהַטַּעַם מִפְּנֵי מִדָּה זוֹ כִּי חָפֵץ חֶסֶד הוּא רוֹצֶה בַּמֶּה שֶׁיִּשְׂרָאֵל גּוֹמְלִים חֶסֶד וְאוֹתוֹ

צַד מַזְכִּיר לָהֶם עִם הֱיוֹת שֶׁאֵינָם כְּשֵׁרִים בְּצַד אַחֵר.

אִם כֵּן בְּמִדָּה זוֹ רָאוּי הָאָדָם לְהִתְנַהֵג אַף אִם יִרְאֶה שֶׁאָדָם עוֹשֶׂה לוֹ רַע וּמַכְעִיסוֹ אִם יֵשׁ בּוֹ צַד טוֹבָה שֶׁמֵּטִיב לַאֲחֵרִים אוֹ מִדָּה טוֹבָה שֶׁמִּתְנַהֵג כַּשּׁוּרָה יַסְפִּיק לוֹ צַד זֶה לְבַטֵּל כַּעֲסוֹ מֵעָלָיו וְיֵרָצֶה לָבוֹא עִמּוֹ וְיַחְפֹּץ חֶסֶד וְיֹאמַר דַּי לִי בְּטוֹבָה זוֹ שֶׁיֵּשׁ לוֹ וְכָל שֶׁכֵּן בְּאִשְׁתּוֹ כִּדְפֵרְשׁוּ רַבּוֹתֵינוּ זִכְרוֹנָם לִבְרָכָה דַּיֵּנוּ שֶׁמְּגַדְּלוֹת אֶת בָּנֵינוּ וּמַצִּילוֹת אוֹתָנוּ מִן הַחֵטְא, כָּךְ יֹאמַר עַל כָּל אָדָם דַּי לִי בְּטוֹבָה פְּלוֹנִית שֶׁעָשָׂה לִי אוֹ שֶׁעָשָׂה עִם פְּלוֹנִי אוֹ מִדָּה טוֹבָה פְּלוֹנִית שֶׁיֵּשׁ לוֹ וְיִהְיֶה חָפֵץ חֶסֶד:

The Sixth Level

For He Desires Kindness

I have explained elsewhere that there is a certain chamber where angels are appointed to collect the acts of kindness that people perform in this world. When Justice denounces the Jewish people, these angels immediately produce a particular act of kindness, and God forgives the Jews. This is because *He desires kindness*. Even if they are guilty, if they nevertheless do kindness with one another, God forgives them. This is as it was during the destruction of the Temple. God told the angel Gabriel, *go into the space of the* galgal. Gabriel took burning coals to cast upon the Jewish people. Gabriel, the officer of justice and power, was given permission from God to take the forces of Justice from the *galgal*, located below the cherubim, forces derived from the fires of the altar, the executive power of justice through sovereignty. Justice demanded the destruction of absolutely everything, extinguishing the future of the Jewish people because they deserved annihilation. The passage continues, *and Gabriel looked to the cherubim, and under their wings he saw the form of a human hand.* God said to Gabriel: "They do kindness to one another. Even though they are undeserving, save them and allow a remnant to remain." The reason is because of this Level, *for He desires kindness.* The Jewish people perform acts of kindness, and this stands to their merit, even if they are not worthy in some other aspect.

If so, then this Level is appropriate for people to adopt. Even if a person does harm and angers another, as long as the offender has some positive aspect—helping others, for example, or some other proper behavior—then that positive behavior should be sufficient to nullify one's anger, achieve reconciliation, and even good will. A person should say, "It is enough for me that this person performs this one kindness." This is especially true regarding one's spouse, as the Rabbis of Blessed Memory taught, "it is enough for us that our spouses raise our children and rescue us from sin." A person should say, "it is enough for me that this person did me a certain kindness, or did a certain kindness for someone else, or has a certain good quality." In this manner a person may emulate *for He desires kindness.*

Commentary

The Book of Ezekiel, suffused with mystical content, is the starting place for the Sixth Level of Mercy. Rabbi Cordovero refers readers to a passage in his *Pardes Rimonim* (Sha'ar Heikhalot 5), and then delves deeper into the meaning of events described in Ezekiel 10. Gabriel, the archangel of Justice whose very essence is derived from the *sefirah* of *Gevurah*, receives a command by God to descend to the world and bring destruction and ruin upon the Jewish people. The elemental power for this calamity rests in the fiery heat of the *galgal*, a space in the Temple below the winged angelic creatures known as the cherubim. According to the Midrash (*Vayikra Rabah* 26:8) Gabriel takes hold of these glowing coals and readies himself to cast them upon the Jewish people, but God stays his hand for an incredible six years, waiting to see if the Jews would repent.

Rabbi Epstein explains the workings of Divine Justice as a gradual descent of the Will of God through the four worlds of *atsilut, beriyah, yetsirah* and *asiyah*. As Justice moves through each of these worlds, it is transformed into a being more suited its new conditions (in Kabbalistic parlance, it is clothed in garments appropriate for each world) until it finally reaches *asiyah*, the world of action that we perceive. Here, Justice is clothed in things that we recognize: famine, pestilence, war. Moreover, each of the four worlds has its own structure of ten *sefirot*, such that *Malkhut*, the lowest *sefirah* of the highest world of *atsilut*, aligns with *Keter*, the highest *sefirah* of the lower world of *beriyah*. By the time Justice travels through the ten *sefirot* of each of the four worlds, coming to rest in *Malkhut* of *asiyah*, it finds expression in completely mundane entities, animate or otherwise: the locust that despoils the grain, a lethal virus, a hand grenade.

Gabriel's direct involvement in the process represents an especially strict expression of the execution of punishment, known to Kabbalists as Justice through Sovereignty (*gevurat ha-malkhut*). The *sefirot* are not static, fixed entities. Their movement alters the manner in which Divine energy flows into the Universe. Contrast, for example, the way electricity flows into your home with the way a lightning bolt crashes through the night sky. The former is a regular expression of human engineering, harnessing the power of the generator and channeling it through municipal conduits and transformers, directing it through meters and along copper wires to the outlets on your walls. As long as everything is functioning normally, the electricity is both plentiful and regular. Lightning, on the other hand, is a huge explosion of energy that seeks its ground directly from its source to its destination, careening through the atmosphere with only mild and sporadic resistance from the vagaries of the air. Both are expressions of the power of electricity, but whereas one is controlled and predictable, utilized for beneficial purpose, the other unleashes great and immediate destruction.

So too the channeling of Divine energy. When human beings comport themselves properly, the *sefirot* remain in their intended alignment: the *sefirot* on the left, representing Justice (*gevurah* and *hod*) balance the *sefirot* on the right, representing Mercy (*hesed* and *netsah*). The right and the left, Justice and Mercy, are then filtered through the *sefirot* that remain in the center (*tiferet* and *yesod*), finally expressing themselves in *malkhut*. Human choice affects the delicate balance of the *sefirot*. In the Sixth Level of Mercy, Rabbi Cordovero mentions a potentially disastrous alignment of the *sefirot*, occasioned by human transgression—*gevurat ha-malkhut*, or Justice through Sovereignty—in which the energy flowing from Justice (*Gevurah*) is not mediated by mixing with the powers of

Mercy through *Tiferet* and *Yesod*, rather it flows directly from its source in *Gevurah* to its destination *Malkhut*, wreaking horrible devastation on the world. To borrow from the electrical metaphor above, this would be like allowing the energy created in a nuclear plant to flow directly into a home and household appliances without any mediation or moderation to the correct voltage.

Thus Gabriel's descent to the *galgal* to remove the glowing coals of *Gevurah* represented a potentially devastating act. God, however, employed the Sixth Level of Mercy to stay Divine anger, in two specific ways. First, as the Midrash relates, God delayed the implementation of this decree by a remarkable six years, leaving Gabriel standing with the coals in his hand, waiting for the signal to rain destruction on the Jewish people. Metaphorically, this gave God time, as it were, to look for whatever redeeming characteristics the Jewish people might possess, such that God could justify the cancellation of the decree (these anthropomorphisms are clearly intended for human benefit—God, Whose wisdom is infinite and absolute, certainly does not need time to make a decision, yet such Divine behavior provides a powerful object lesson to the human intellect). Second, God provided a sign for Gabriel: the image of the hand, representing human kindness. Recalling this redeeming characteristic, God is able to modify his original intent of absolute destruction, employing the Sixth Level of Mercy to forgive the Jewish people. The midrash continues with God saying, "Gabriel, Gabriel—there are some people among them who give charity to others," and the mission of destruction is cancelled. Whatever their faults, the Jewish people are kind to one another and this is enough to stay the powers of annihilation.

The theological analysis of this passage betrays an

apparent contradiction: if God sent Gabriel to administer the punishment determined by justice, how is it that God should reverse that decision by alluding to kindness, which exercises the faculty of mercy? This can only be understood as an object lesson in the mechanism of forgiveness: God keeps a reserve of redeeming characteristics at hand as a failsafe against Divine anger, calling upon this reserve when the behavior of the Jewish people elicits a consequence of punishment. These redeeming characteristics—in this case, human kindness as represented by the hand—are kept in a "certain chamber," and this chamber is always accessed before Divine judgment is visited upon humanity. The chamber, however, must be filled in advance.

So it is with human interaction. Perhaps the people who anger us most are those we deal with most frequently, at home, work or school. To master the Sixth Level of Mercy, it is essential that we take some time to reflect on the redeeming characteristics of everyone around us (and especially those closest to us) and then commit those characteristics to memory. These characteristics need not be huge acts of spiritual heroism; they may be simple things like "she always makes my lunch" or "he always takes out the garbage." It may even be useful to create a mental avatar for such things, such as an image of a lunchbox or a clean garbage can. When the inevitable moments of conflict arise, and we are tempted to lash out in frustration, then we must go into that "chamber" and look around at whatever avatars come to mind. The value of taking out the garbage may not be anywhere near in significance to the offense that flares our temper, but the value of taking a moment to pause and disassociate from the steadily building fury gives us the space to modify our responses carefully. God, as it were, took six years to consider his decision to destroy the Jewish people, leaving

Gabriel holding onto the glowing coals all the while. We can certainly pause and reflect before we vent our anger on those we love.

Rabbi Cordovero concludes with a remarkably candid and personal observation, rarely identified in *Date Palm of Devorah*: this Sixth Level is especially valuable for spouses. He provides a reference to a Talmudic passage regarding Rabbi Hiyya and his wife (*Yevamot* 63a). It seems that she was an especially difficult woman, frequently berating him over one thing or another, perpetually dissatisfied and bitter. The Talmud records that "whenever he found something that she would value, he wrapped it up in a cloth and brought it to her," yet she remained unappreciative and prone to petty acts of spite. When asked why Rabbi Hiyyah was so careful to render these kindnesses when his wife did not reciprocate, he answered, "it is enough for us that they raise our children, and that they save us from sin," meaning, his wife took care of their family, and shared intimacy with her husband. His response is precisely the Sixth Level: he identified a kindness that his wife engaged in, and recalling these positive attributes, he was able to forgo his anger with her inappropriate behavior. Rabbi Cordovero urges us to store up such elements in the *galgal*, so that they may serve as a temporary stop to ill-planned outbursts, and contribute to family harmony. This strategy will not solve deeper issues of conflict, but will act as a prophylactic measure to prevent an escalation of animosity.

Perhaps one might object to Rabbi Hiyyah's line of reasoning, arguing that his wife was acting purely out of her own selfishness. After all, the children were hers as well, and intimacy is beneficial to both partners. Rabbi Epstein cites Rabbi Mikhl Zilber in response to this objection, saying that we should not be overly demanding when it comes to the intent of a kind deed. "One who loses a coin which is found by a poor person is considered to have donated charity," he writes, and illustrates this concept with a Talmudic teaching (*Berakhot* 28): "a good guest, what does he say? See how much effort the host expended for me! A bad guest, what does he say? What effort did the host expend? Whatever effort he expended, he only did so for his wife and children. Even though this may be true, that the host did not expend effort except for his wife and children." Rabbi Epstein continues, "even a storekeeper who works to make a profit, receives a kindness from his customers. Even his employee deserves his gratitude, for even though he is paid as compensation for his labor, behold in the end the employee nevertheless provides sustenance and a livelihood for the employer." In other words, it is more productive for us to recognize the benefits we receive from others than it is to probe the motivations for their actions. If we wish to master the Sixth Level of Mercy, we must focus on those benefits we receive from others, cultivating gratitude as a perpetual state of mind.

Practical Applications

Abigail's father has such a critical attitude! It's impossible to tell him anything about her life without getting an earful of criticism. It's not that he dislikes everything she do, it's just that he always focusses on the first negative thing that he finds, and can't manage to find praise until he exhausts his disapproval of that fly in the ointment. She told him about a young man she recently dated, for example, and true to form, the only thing he could say was that the young man wasn't sufficiently ambitious.

Abigail knows that this negativity is simply his way of demonstrating that he wants the best for her, but she needs an additional tool to hold back a biting retort. Luckily, she's been reading *Date Palm of Devorah,* and she recalls the Sixth Level. She remembers how her father worked hard to provide for her orthodontic treatment as a child, and she's especially proud of her straight, white teeth. She creates an image in her mind of her own bright smile, and thinks of how hard he worked to pay for those braces, and this cools her anger enough to speak calmly with her father.

David shares an office with Saul, and the relationship is frequently tense: David recognizes that he is a neat-freak, while his coworker is an absolute slob. He can't file anything, and his desk is piled high with important papers that threaten to topple over at any minute. Post-it notes and other reminders as pasted all over his computer, lamp, and telephone in a chaotic fashion, and David shudders when he thinks of Saul's lack of organization. What's worse, it doesn't even seem to bother Saul, which is something David simply can't comprehend. David has been doing his best to ignore Saul's mess, but it's been getting harder and harder every day—just walking into the office and seeing his clutter drives David up the wall with frustration.

An advanced student of *Date Palm of Devorah*, David knows that he is liable to explode over this issue at some point, and so he's been working on himself for weeks to avoid a disaster. Thinking of the hand in the *galgal*, David has spent some time meditating on Saul's redeeming characteristics, and has created an avatar to readily remind himself of the best things in Saul's personality. David has noticed that Saul is especially generous with his coworkers, a trait that is sorely missing in their corporate culture. He's always available to help others with any issue, solving minor computer problems and staying late to help someone meet an urgent deadline. David remembers one report that Saul submitted to the Vice President in which Saul kindly acknowledged David's participation in the research—David even received an email from the VP, thanking him for his role in the work, even though it was very minor. The avatar of Saul's redeeming characteristic of generosity is the cover of that report.

When David walked into the office that Monday morning, his frustration with Saul immediately rose to the boiling point. There Saul was, feet up on his desk as he talked with someone on the phone, ignoring the huge pile of papers that had evidently fallen onto the floor. How could he be so oblivious to the mess around him? David was tempted to hang up the call in the middle of Saul's conversation, and let him have it once and for all! Still, he recognized that the moment for the Sixth Level of Mercy had come, and he forced himself to contemplate the cover of Saul's report that generated the email from the VP, and his anger slowly dissipated. David was able to control himself sufficiently to walk over to his own desk and wait for Saul to finish the conversation before he spoke to him gently about how disturbed he was by the mess in the office.

The Seventh Level: A Knot is Stronger

Introduction

Rabbi Cordovero begins the Seventh Level of Mercy with a well-known teaching of the Talmud (*Berakhot* 34b): "in a place where penitents stand, not even the completely righteous may stand," a statement that counterintuitively affirms the power of repentance—not only is the penitent accepted back into Divine favor, the penitent is drawn still closer than before the transgression. Rabbi Cordovero derives the reason for this phenomenon from another Talmudic passage connected to the Hebrew letter *he* (pronounced "hey"), which is shaped like a kind of covered patio: roofed overhead, a wall to the right, a half-wall to the left, and open at the bottom (ה). The repentance process takes place when a person falls out the bottom of the *he*. It is impossible to climb back along the same path of descent; rather the penitent must ascend on the outside of the letter, finally entering through the tiny opening at the top left. This arduous process gives the penitent greater strength, and renders the penitent more beloved to God than even the completely righteous.

From the human perspective, the Seventh Level of Mercy addresses the damage done to a relationship through betrayal. Even after tearful apologies are spoken and accepted, the natural tendency is to hold back a certain degree of affection or respect as a result of prior harm, regardless of how intensely and sincerely the other may repent. The Seventh Level dictates that not only should the relationship be restored to its earlier strength, it should even be improved as a result of the commitment to renewal.

השביעית - יָשׁוּב יְרַחֲמֵנוּ

הִנֵּה אֵין הַבּ"ה מִתְנַהֵג כְּמִדַּת בָּשָׂר וָדָם שֶׁאִם הִכְעִיסוֹ חֲבֵרוֹ כְּשֶׁהוּא מִתְרַצֶּה עִמּוֹ מִתְרַצֶּה מְעַט לֹא כְּאַהֲבָה הַקּוֹדֶמֶת. אֲבָל אִם חָטָא אָדָם וְעָשָׂה תְּשׁוּבָה, מַעֲלָתוֹ יוֹתֵר גְּדוֹלָה עִם הַבּ"ה, וְהַיְנוּ בְּמָקוֹם שֶׁבַּעֲלֵי תְּשׁוּבָה עוֹמְדִים אֵין צַדִּיקִים גְּמוּרִים יְכוֹלִין לַעֲמוֹד. וְהַטַּעַם כִּדְפֵרְשׁוּ בְּפֶרֶק הַבּוֹנֶה בְּעִנְיַן ה' לָמָּה הִיא עֲשׂוּיָה כְּאַכְסַדְרָא שֶׁכָּל הָרוֹצֶה לָצֵאת מֵעוֹלָמוֹ יֵצֵא.

פֵּרוּשׁ הָעוֹלָם נִבְרָא בַּה' וְהַבּ"ה בָּרָא הָעוֹלָם פָּתוּחַ לְצַד הָרַע וְהַחֵטְא לִרְוָחָה וְאֵין צַד שֶׁאֵין חֹמֶר וְיֵצֶר הָרַע וּפְגָם כְּמִין אַכְסַדְרָא, אֵינוֹ בַּעַל גְּדָרִים אֶלָּא פִּרְצָה גְּדוֹלָה פְּרוּצָה לְצַד הָרַע לְצַד מַטָּה כָּל מִי שֶׁיִּרְצֶה לָצֵאת מֵעוֹלָמוֹ כַּמָּה פְּתָחִין לוֹ לֹא יִפְנֶה לְצַד שֶׁלֹּא יִמְצָא צַד חֵטְא וְעָוֹן לִכָּנֵס אֶל הַחִיצוֹנִים, וְהִיא פְּתוּחָה מִלְּמַעְלָה שֶׁאִם יָשׁוּב יְקַבְּלוּהוּ. וְהִקְשׁוּ וּלְהַדְרוּהוּ בְּהַאי, לֹא מִסְתַּיְּעָא מִלְּתָא.

רָצוּ בָּזֶה שֶׁהַשָּׁב בִּתְשׁוּבָה לֹא יַסְפִּיק לוֹ שֶׁיִּהְיֶה נִגְדָּר בְּעָוֹן בְּגֶדֶר הַצַּדִּיקִים מִפְּנֵי שֶׁהַצַּדִּיקִים שֶׁלֹּא חָטְאוּ גֶּדֶר מְעַט יַסְפִּיק אֲלֵיהֶם אָמְנָם הַחוֹטֵא שֶׁחָטָא וְשָׁב לֹא יַסְפִּיק לוֹ גֶּדֶר מְעַט אֶלָּא צָרִיךְ לְהַגְדִּיר עַצְמוֹ כַּמָּה גְּדָרִים קָשִׁים מִפְּנֵי שֶׁאוֹתוֹ

הַגָּדֵר הַמְעַט כְּבָר נִפְרַץ פַּעַם אַחַת אִם יִתְקָרֵב שָׁם בְּקַל יִפְתָּהוּ יִצְרוֹ אֶלָּא צָרִיךְ לְהִתְרַחֵק הַרְחֵק גָּדוֹל מְאֹד, וְלָזֶה לֹא יִכָּנֵס דֶּרֶךְ פֶּתַח הָאַכְסַדְרָא שֶׁהַפִּרְצָה שָׁם אֶלָּא יִתְעַלֶּה וְיִכָּנֵס דֶּרֶךְ פֶּתַח צַר וְיַעֲשֶׂה כַּמָּה צָרוֹת וְסִגּוּפִים לְעַצְמוֹ וְיִסְתֹּם הַפְּרָצוֹת. וּמִטַּעַם זֶה בְּמָקוֹם שֶׁבַּעֲלֵי תְּשׁוּבָה עוֹמְדִים וְכוּ' מִפְּנֵי שֶׁלֹּא נִכְנְסוּ דֶּרֶךְ פֶּתַח הַצַּדִּיקִים כְּדֵי שֶׁיִּהְיוּ עִם הַצַּדִּיקִים, אֶלָּא נִצְטַעֲרוּ וְעָלוּ דֶּרֶךְ פֶּתַח הָעֶלְיוֹן וְסִגְּפוּ עַצְמָן וְנִבְדְּלוּ מִן הַחֵטְא יוֹתֵר וְיוֹתֵר מִן הַצַּדִּיקִים לְכָךְ עָלוּ וְעָמְדוּ בְּמַדְרֵגַת ה' הֵיכָל חֲמִישִׁי שֶׁבְּגַן עֵדֶן דְּהַיְנוּ גַּג הֵה"א וְצַדִּיקִים בְּפֶתַח הַהֵ"א בִּכְנִיסַת הָאַכְסַדְרָא וְלָזֶה כַּאֲשֶׁר הָאָדָם יַעֲשֶׂה תְּשׁוּבָה דְּהַיְנוּ תָּשׁוּב ה' אֶל מְקוֹמָהּ, וְיַחֲזִיר הַבָּ"ה שְׁכִינָתוֹ עָלָיו אֵינוֹ שָׁב בְּאַהֲבָה הָרִאשׁוֹנָה בִּלְבַד, אֶלָּא יוֹתֵר וְיוֹתֵר. וְהַיְנוּ יָשׁוּב יְרַחֲמֵנוּ יוֹסִיף רַחֲמִים לְיִשְׂרָאֵל וִיתַקְּנֵם וִיקָרְבֵם יוֹתֵר.

וְכָךְ הָאָדָם צָרִיךְ לְהִתְנַהֵג עִם חֲבֵרוֹ לֹא יִהְיֶה נוֹטֵר אֵיבָה מֵהַכַּעַס הַקּוֹדֵם אֶלָּא כְּשֶׁיִּרְאֶה שֶׁחֲבֵרוֹ מְבַקֵּשׁ אַהֲבָתוֹ יִהְיֶה לוֹ בְּמַדְרֵגַת רַחֲמִים וְאַהֲבָה יוֹתֵר וְיוֹתֵר מִקֹּדֶם וְיֹאמַר הֲרֵי הוּא לִי כְּבַעֲלֵי תְּשׁוּבָה שֶׁאֵין צַדִּיקִים גְּמוּרִים יְכוֹלִים לַעֲמֹד אֶצְלָם וִיקָרְבֵהוּ תַּכְלִית קִרְבָה יוֹתֵר מִמַּה שֶּׁהוּא

מְקָרֵב אֹתָם שֶׁהֵם צַדִּיקִים גְּמוּרִים עִמּוֹ שֶׁלֹּא חָטְאוּ אֶצְלוֹ:

The Seventh Level

He will again show mercy

God does not behave as human beings behave. After someone angers another, forgiveness is usually partial and they do not love each other as they once did. When a person sins and repents, however, God holds him in even higher regard. This is as it is written: "the place where penitents stand, not even the completely righteous may stand." The reason is explained in the Talmud regarding the Hebrew letter *he* (ה). Why is it shaped like a covered patio? This to teach us that anyone who wishes to leave this world may leave.

God created the world created with the letter *he*. God created it with a wide bottom facing the side of evil and sin, a side that cannot be free of materialism, the desire to do evil, and imperfection. This is like a covered patio. There is no protective fence below, just a great opening to the side of evil. If one wishes to leave this world—there are so many exits for such a person, and one cannot turn without encountering sin and transgression, an opening to the outside. There is also an upper opening, such that if a person returns, he or she will be accepted. One might ask, "Let the person return the same way?" The answer is "this would not help."

The penitent cannot rely on standard defenses against sin as the righteous may. Since the righteous have not sinned, a light fence is sufficient for them. A sinner, on the other hand, needs robust and multiple fences, since the light fence has already been destroyed. If one were to approach this fence, it would easily be destroyed again by the evil inclination. Such a person needs to maintain maximum distance. Therefore it would be insufficient for such a person to re-enter the patio in the way he exited. He must climb up and enter via the small opening, and suffering and self-denial will seal up the gaps. For this reason, "the place where penitents stand" is higher because they did not enter via the portal of the righteous to be with the righteous. Rather, they mortified themselves and rose up to the higher opening, practicing self-denial and separating from sin so much more than the righteous. Therefore they rise up and stand in the level of the *he*, the fifth chamber of *he* that is in the Garden of Eden. This is called "the roof of the *he*." The righteous, meanwhile, are in the opening of the *he*, the entrance to the patio. Thus when a person repents, this brings the *he* back into its place, returning the *Shekhinah* to God. This return is not characterized by the earlier love alone, rather a far deeper love. This is the meaning of "He will again show mercy," that God will invest greater mercy in the Jewish people, healing them and drawing them closer.

So too should people behave with one another. One should not retain the hatred from an earlier anger. Rather, when a person sees that someone desires love, the level of mercy should be increased and love should be deepened to an even greater degree than before. One should say, "behold, this person is to me as a penitent, and even the completely righteous cannot stand in his or her company." One should draw the penitent close with the greatest of affection, even more than one would lavish on the completely righteous, who never gave offense.

Commentary

In his commentary on the *Zohar* (*Bereshit* 5:1) Rabbi Cordovero identifies three distinct types of repentance (*teshuvah*). The first is *teshuvat ha-mishkal,* or "repentance of weighing," in which the penitent identifies exactly how much benefit he or she received through the sin and attempts to expiate it through self-induced suffering. This form of repentance may have been well-represented in certain movements throughout Jewish history such as the Hasidei Ashkenaz of 13th-century Germany, but many prominent thinkers in the modern era have decidedly discouraged people from following this path (see for example the 18th-century Rabbi Moshe Hayim Luzzatto in *Mesilat Yesharim,* and the 20th century responsum of Rabbi Moshe Feinstein as published in the Feldheim edition of *Orhot Tsadikim*). The second form of *teshuvah,* according to Rabbi Cordovero, is "repentance of the future" (*teshuvat ha-ba*), in which a person successfully withstands a moral challenge in an area of prior weakness. Maimonides refers to such an individual as a "complete Master of Repentance" (*ba'al teshuvah gemurah,* see his Laws of Repentance 2:1). Other than with a firm and absolute resolution to avoid sin, however, it is difficult to understand how one prepares to achieve "repentance of the future." The third type of *teshuvah* is especially relevant to Level Seven. Rabbi Cordovero calls the third type "repentance of the fence" (*teshuvat ha-geder*), and it refers to the creation of "fences" to avoid transgression. Just as a fence protects a property from interlopers, accidental or otherwise, so too do carefully chosen behavior modifications protect a person from sin.

Rabbi Cordovero cites a passage in the Talmud in a chapter entitled *Ha-boneh* (*Shabat* 104a) regarding the meaning of the shapes of the letters of the Hebrew alphabet to illustrate his understanding of *teshuvah* (see also *Menahot* 29b). The letter *he* alludes to the process of repentance, *teshuvah:* the very purpose of this world is repentance, a concept which is borne out by the very shape of the letter.

The Aramaic term *aksadra* (based on the Greek word "exedra") describes an outdoor roofed area that has a low wall on one side, much like a balcony or porch, like the Hebrew letter *he* (ה). The right hand "wall" of the letter *he* is like the back of the *aksadra*, the left hand wall is like the railing in front of the porch or balcony, and the horizontal line at the top of the letter is like the roof of the balcony. The metaphor becomes a little awkward in one key aspect: unlike an actual balcony, the letter *he* does not have a "floor." If it were an actual balcony, anyone who stepped out onto it would immediately fall through, a significant architectural weakness.

For the metaphor, however, the potential of falling out the bottom is crucial, since it refers to human sin. In our context, falling out the bottom of the *he* is understood as a form of betrayal, whether it be a betrayal of God, of those we love, or even ourselves. Once we fall out the bottom, it becomes very difficult to get back inside the walls of the *he* again. Moreover, even if one were to climb back up into the *he* by following one's tracks, it would be very easy to collapse once again along the same path.

Consider, for example, an alcoholic who has integrated his addiction into his daily routine by stopping at a bar on the way home from work, drinking far too much, and then staggering home past a late-night liquor store where he picks up a bottle for consumption at home. If he manages, with great effort, to wean himself off his terrible habit, he will be faced with the same challenges at the close of every workday when he makes his way home, passing by his favorite bar and the convenient liquor store. In order to effectively reform himself, therefore, he must take an alternate route home, avoiding the places that he regularly frequented, even though it may be a much longer and more arduous journey. With every step on this path he demonstrates his dedication to sobriety.

The analogy of one who falls out of the *he* is similar. He cannot simply decide to retrace his steps straight up, because he would easily fall out along a path that he has already described. He must rather find an alternate, more difficult route along the outside side of the *he*, working his way upward until he can enter the small opening at the top left of the letter (ה). His effort is greater, and in fact he must elevate himself to the very top of the letter, the "roof" of the *he*. The constant dedication and effort demonstrates a great level of commitment to reform, and thus he is more beloved for his hard work. Ironically, his earlier failure makes his relationship with his Creator stronger, not weaker.

Rabbi Eliyahu deVidas, Rabbi Cordovero's student, uses a beautiful metaphor to explain this phenomenon (*Reshit Hokhmah*, Gate of Repentance 1). In *Date Palm of Devorah*, Rabbi Cordovero alludes to the returning of the *he* to its place, which is understood as establishing the proper relationship of the *sefirot* of *binah* (represented by the letter *he* in the word *teshuvah*) and *tiferet* (the letter *vav*). Rabbi deVidas compares the flow of Divine energy through the *sefirot* to an irrigation pipe that nurtures fields and orchards. Human sin has the effect of creating a misalignment of the parts of the pipe, causing the water to leak out in unintended areas, not reaching the parched young plants. Repairing the breach is essential to the entire growth process, and attending to the problem allows the farmer to reinforce the site of the original damage, making it even stronger than before.

God is present throughout the process, ironically anticipating our transgression and creating the mechanism for *teshuvah* in advance. Rabbi Epstein cites an astounding *midrash* (*Kohelet Iyov* 10) regarding a group of criminals who rebel against the king. They are arrested and thrown into prison, but they manage to dig a tunnel and escape. One of them, however, does not flee with the others, and in the morning he is discovered by the king. "Fool," says the king, "freedom is before you, and you did not flee!" So too, continues the *midrash*, does God say to the wicked: "*teshuvah* is before you, and you did not repent!" The opening in the letter *he*, writes Rabbi Epstein, is the escape tunnel.

The Talmud records an interesting debate between Rabbi Abahu and Rabbi Yohanan (*Berakhot* 34b). Rabbi Abahu states, "a place a penitent stands—not even the perfectly righteous may stand," citing a verse to prove his point. Rabbi Yohanan, on the other hand, maintains that Rabbi Abahu has misunderstood the verse in question. A correct reading of the verse reveals quite the opposite: those who have never sinned in their lives stand in a place that remains beyond the reach of ordinary people. Maimonides, and most of the later authorities, rule in favor of Rabbi Abahu: one who has sinned and repented demonstrates a spiritual superiority to someone who has never sinned at all.

The implications for human relationships are profound: the bond between people may actually become stronger if it has been tested by a betrayal. In other words, if a friend wronged you in some way and then sincerely and completely repented, the surviving friendship ultimately demonstrates far greater resilience. This depends, at least in part, on the spiritual strength of the one who was wronged. Can the friend be forgiven after an act of such magnitude? According to Rabbi Cordovero, the Seventh Level describes God's ability to forgive those who repent, even to the extent that they are cherished even more than those who have never sinned at all.

Forgiveness, however, should not be confused with forgetfulness. Sin has lasting consequences that remain even after forgiveness. Scripture illustrates such consequences in the relationships between God and human beings in numerous places. King David, for example, sincerely repented his behavior surrounding Batsheva and her husband Uriah, but God nevertheless meted out a terrible and permanent punishment through David's offspring (Samuel II: 11-12). The Torah also sets limits to forgiveness in the example of an unfaithful spouse: although the couple may reconcile, a single act of infidelity may render their continued marriage impossible. The concept discussed in the Seventh Level does not shed light on the *halakhic* implications of sin and repentance. The focus here examines the proper perspective of the one who was wronged: how should a person process the deeply felt regret of the one who committed the betrayal? The Seventh Level demands that one regard the sincerely repentant person with a paradoxically greater love than ever before.

In the Third Level ("Take Care of it Personally"), Rabbi Goldberg and Rabbi Shaynberg presented differing opinions regarding the posture of the penitent. According to Rabbi Goldberg, God only fully cleanses the penitent of sin when the repentance is done out of love, whereas Rabbi Shaynberg maintained that even the lower level of repentance out of fear was sufficient. It remains to be seen if this difference may be maintained in the Seventh Level.

On a human level, certainly we should extend this exceptional level of forgiveness to someone who sincerely regrets harming us because they have respect and admiration for us. Are we also obligated to forgive someone who regrets harming us because we have the power to harm him as well? *Date Palm of Devorah* is not clear on this point, although perhaps Rabbi Cordovero's use of the phrase "when a person sees that someone desires his love" implies that the Seventh Level applies to penitents who repent out of love, not fear. Repentance out of love is an entirely different phenomenon than repentance out of fear. A son who fears his father will examine his behavior and adapt it to avoid detection and possible punishment. A son who loves his father, on the other hand, will examine his behavior with a view to improving his ability to please his father. Love inherently inspires the son to be proactive, thinking "what can I do to bring my father joy?" rather than "how may I avoid displeasing my father?"

There is a popular saying to the effect that a knot is stronger than a string that has never been severed. Not only that—a rope, once retied in a knot, brings the extreme ends of closer to each other than they were before the breach. The Seventh Level reinforces this image: we are encouraged to not only repair our relationships, but to draw still closer to those who wish our forgiveness.

Practical Applications

"I messed up," says Leon's teenage son, "and I know it." The damage isn't really so bad, and after all, that's what automobile insurance is for anyway. Still, Leon carefully examines the ruined fender to really drive the point home. "You told me to be especially careful in parking lots, and I wasn't. I'm really sorry." He's embarrassed and ashamed. Leon gives him his most serious, stern look and says nothing.

Okay, that's enough.

Leon puts his arm around his son's shoulders, tells him it's alright, and tells him how he felt when he had his first fender-bender. Leon sets some limits on the use of the car, but shows him a generosity of spirit and draws him closer than he ever was before.

The Eighth Level: Maintain a Core of Love

Rabbi Cordovero expands upon the metaphysics of forgiveness in the Eighth Level. God preserves a core region of positive regard for every human being, a place where every positive deed that person ever performed is recalled, cherished, and protected. Even when a person commits some act of transgression, the impact of that inappropriate behavior cannot affect the core of love. In other words, God does not keep a running tally of pros and cons regarding each individual, subtracting the blame for transgressions from the reward for good deeds to assess a type of score for each individual. Rather, God is like a king who maintains two halls for his servants. One is beautifully decorated, filled with luxurious furnishings under a lofty ceiling and illuminated with chandeliers. In this hall, servants are received and rewarded for performing the king's will, and the king frequently returns to this hall to review the record books and rejoice in the memory of their contributions to the kingdom. The second hall is a plain room, devoid of any luxuries, in which the king reviews the records of servants who have failed to perform their duties appropriately, and they receive punishment. The kingdom has yet to see a servant who is not called to both chambers, yet the king maintains a strict policy: no misdeeds are to be mentioned in the glorious hall of reward.

So too, God maintains a chamber where the positive actions of a person are stored, and no matter how poorly a person may behave, he or she will never lose their place in this holy chamber. Rabbi Cordovero describes the meaning of this Level, and provides direction on how we may apply it in our own lives.

השמינית - יִכְבּשׁ עֲוֹנוֹתֵינוּ

הֲרֵי הקב"ה מִתְנַהֵג עִם יִשְׂרָאֵל בְּמִדָּה זוֹ וְהִיא סוֹד כְּבִישַׁת הֶעָוֹן. כִּי הִנֵּה הַמִּצְווֹת הִיא כְּפוֹרַחַת עָלְתָה נִצָּהּ וּבוֹקַעַת וְעוֹלָה עַד אֵין תַּכְלִית לְכָנֵס לְפָנָיו יִתְבָּרַךְ אָמְנָם הָעֲוֹנוֹת אֵין לָהֶם כְּנִיסָה שָׁם ח"ו אֶלָּא כְּבָשָׁם שֶׁלֹּא יִכָּנְסוּ כְּדִכְתִיב לֹא יְגֻרְךָ רָע לֹא יָגוּר בִּמְגוּרְךָ רָע.

אִם כֵּן אֵין הֶעָוֹן נִכְנָס פְּנִימָה. וּמִטַּעַם זֶה שְׂכַר מִצְוָה בְּהַאי עָלְמָא לֵיכָּא מִפְּנֵי שֶׁהֵם לְפָנָיו יִתְבָּרַךְ וְהַאֵיךְ יִתֵּן לוֹ מִמַּה שֶׁלְּפָנָיו שְׂכַר רוּחָנִי בָּעוֹלָם גַּשְׁמִי וַהֲרֵי כָּל הָעוֹלָם אֵינוֹ כְּדַאי לְמִצְוָה אַחַת וּלְקוֹרַת רוּחַ אֲשֶׁר לְפָנָיו. וּמִטַּעַם זֶה לֹא יִקַּח שׁוֹחַד שֶׁל מִצְווֹת, הַמָּשָׁל בָּזֶה, אֵין הקב"ה אוֹמֵר עָשָׂה אַרְבָּעִים מִצְווֹת וְעֶשֶׂר עֲבֵרוֹת נִשְׁאֲרוּ שְׁלֹשִׁים מִצְווֹת וְיֵלְכוּ עֶשֶׂר בְּעֶשֶׂר חַס וְשָׁלוֹם אֶלָּא אֲפִלּוּ צַדִּיק גָּמוּר וְעָשָׂה עֲבֵרָה אַחַת דּוֹמֶה לְפָנָיו כְּאִלּוּ שָׂרַף אֶת הַתּוֹרָה עַד שֶׁיְּרַצֶּה חֶבְיוֹ וְאַחַר כָּךְ יְקַבֵּל שְׂכַר כָּל מִצְווֹתָיו. וְזֶה חֶסֶד גָּדוֹל שֶׁהשי"ת עוֹשֶׂה עִם הַצַּדִּיקִים שֶׁאֵינוֹ מְנַכֶּה מִפְּנֵי שֶׁהַמִּצְווֹת חֲשׁוּבוֹת מְאֹד וּמִתְעַלּוֹת עַד לְפָנָיו יִתְבָּרַךְ, וְהַאֵיךְ יְנַכֶּה מֵהֶן

בִּשְׁבִיל הָעֲבֵרוֹת כִּי שְׂכַר הָעֲבֵרָה הוּא מְחֻלָּק גֵּיהִנֹּם מֵהַנִּבְזֶה, וְהַמִּצְוֹת שֶׁכָּרָן מֵהַנִּכְבָּד זִיו שְׁכִינָה, וְהֵיאָךְ יְנַכֶּה אֵלּוּ כְּנֶגֶד אֵלּוּ אֶלָּא הב"ה גּוֹבֶה חוֹב הָעֲבֵרוֹת וּמַשְׂכִּיר שְׂכַר כָּל הַמִּצְוֹת. וְהַיְנוּ יִכְבֹּשׁ עֲוֹנוֹתֵינוּ שֶׁאֵין הָעֲוֹנוֹת מִתְגַּבְּרִים לְפָנָיו כְּמִצְוֹת אֶלָּא כּוֹבֵשׁ אוֹתָם שֶׁלֹּא יִתְעַלּוּ וְלֹא יִכָּנְסוּ עִם הֱיוֹת שֶׁהוּא מַשְׁגִּיחַ עַל דַּרְכֵי אִישׁ הַטּוֹב וְהָרַע עִם כָּל זֶה הַטּוֹב אֵינוֹ כּוֹבְשׁוֹ אֶלָּא פּוֹרֵחַ וְעוֹלֶה עַד לִמְאֹד וְנִכְלָל מִצְוָה בְּמִצְוָה וְנִבְנֶה מִמֶּנּוּ בִּנְיָן וּלְבוּשׁ נִכְבָּד וַעֲוֹנוֹת אֵין לָהֶם סְגֻלָּה זוֹ אֶלָּא כּוֹבֵשׁ אוֹתָם שֶׁלֹּא יַצְלִיחוּ הַצְלָחָה זוֹ וְלֹא יִכָּנְסוּ פְּנִימָה.

אַף מִדָּה זוֹ צָרִיךְ הָאָדָם לְהִתְנַהֵג בָּהּ שֶׁלֹּא יִכְבֹּשׁ טוֹבַת חֲבֵרוֹ וְיִזְכּוֹר רָעָתוֹ שֶׁגְּמָלָהוּ אֶלָּא אַדְרַבָּה יִכְבֹּשׁ הָרַע וְיִשְׁכָּחֵהוּ וְיַזְנִיחֵהוּ וְלֹא יָגוּר בִּמְגוּרוֹ רַע וְתִהְיֶה הַטּוֹבָה סְדוּרָה תָּמִיד לְפָנָיו וְיִזְכֹּר לוֹ הַטּוֹבָה וְיַגְבִּיר לוֹ עַל כָּל הַמַּעֲשִׂים שֶׁעָשָׂה לוֹ וְלֹא יְנַכֶּה בְּלִבּוֹ וְיֹאמַר אִם עָשָׂה לִי טוֹבָה הֲרֵי עָשָׂה לִי רָעָה וְיִשְׁכַּח הַטּוֹבָה לֹא יַעֲשֶׂה כֵּן אֶלָּא בְּרָעָה יִתְרַצֶּה כָּל דֶּרֶךְ רָצוּי שֶׁיּוּכַל וְהַטּוֹבָה אַל יַזְנִיחָהּ

לְעוֹלָם מֵבִין עֵינָיו וְיַעֲלִים עֵינוֹ מִן הָרָעָה כָּל מַה שֶׁיּוּכַל כְּדֶרֶךְ שֶׁהב"ה כּוֹבֵשׁ עֲוֹנוֹת כִּדְפֵרַשְׁתִּי:

The Eighth Level

He will Subdue our Transgressions

God behaves toward the Jewish people in accordance with this Level, which is the secret of "subduing the transgression." Behold, a commandment is like a budding vine that bursts forth and rises without limit to enter the very presence of God. Transgressions, on the other hand, do not reach that place, Heaven forbid; rather they are subdued so they do not enter. This is as is written (Psalms 5:5): *no evil will dwell with You*, meaning, no evil will reside in Your dwelling place.

No transgression enters the inner abode. Thus "this world cannot contain the reward for a commandment," because the commandments are before God, and how can God grant people spiritual reward in a physical world? Behold, this entire world is not fit to receive even a kernel of what is before God! For this reason, God does not accept a bribe that consists of the performance of commandments. For example, God does not say, "this person performed forty commandments and ten transgressions. Take ten commandments away for the ten transgressions, leaving thirty commandments." Heaven forbid! Rather, even a completely righteous person who commits a single sin is considered as if he destroyed the Torah. He must make good the debt, and afterward receive the reward for the commandments, which is a great kindness that God does for the righteous. God does not subtract, for observance of the commandments is extremely precious and valued before God—how could God delete the rewards because of transgressions? The consequence of sin is a share of the horrible *Gehinom*, but the reward for the commandments is the glorious radiance of the *Shekhinah*—how could God subtract the former from the latter? Rather, God collects the obligation incurred by the transgressions and provides the reward for the commandments. This is what is meant by "He will subdue our transgressions," that the transgressions do not overpower the commandments. God "subdues" the transgressions so they do not rise up and enter God's presence. Even though God observes all the ways of a person, good and evil, nevertheless God does not subdue the good. God allows the good to fly upward without limit, joining commandment to commandment, building from them an edifice, a garment of glory. Sins do not have this power; rather God subdues them. Sins do not enjoy this success and do not enter the inner presence of God.

Even this Level must be emulated by a human being. One should not subdue the good of a person and recall the evil that he caused. On the contrary, one should subdue the evil, obliterating it from memory and casting it away: *no evil will dwell in Your place*. The good that he did must always be held in consciousness, remembered and overpowering whatever else he might have done. One should not subtract in one's heart, saying, "if he did this good thing for me, behold he also did me harm," forgetting the good. One should not do this! Rather, one should make peace with the harm with whatever means available, and the good should never be cast out of consciousness, while ignoring the evil as much as possible, just as God subdues transgressions, as I have explained.

Commentary

With this Level, Rabbi Cordovero alludes to an important concept in Jewish theology regarding the assessment of reward and punishment. The Talmud records that "the reward for the commandments cannot exist in this world," meaning the spiritual qualities of the reward for positive behavior are too immense to be contained within a finite universe, and therefore must be reserved for the World to Come. This is not to say that God does not provide for more immediate, physical gratification in a material sense, rather the *essence* of the reward is reserved for another realm while the *ancillary* aspects of the reward may be expressed in this world. For example, the daily liturgy includes a passage from the Jerusalem Talmud: "These are the things for which a person receives reward in this world, while the principal reward remains in the world to come…honoring father and mother, acts of kindness, going early to the House of Study morning and evening, receiving guests and visiting the sick, providing for the bride, escorting the dead, intense prayer, bringing peace between people, and the study of Torah is equal to them all." Commandments such as these (the Talmud indicates that they are only a sampling) generate benefits that may be enjoyed immediately, such as the gratitude of honored parents or the entertainment provided by guests. The most important and principal element of the reward for these activities, however, remains waiting in the World to Come.

These rewards, moreover, cannot be nullified. They are placed in an inviolable trust, and cannot be eliminated, no matter how poorly a person behaves in the future. This is what Rabbi Cordovero means by "God does not subtract." One cannot perform a simple calculation like "I have performed forty commandments, and committed ten sins. If God simply takes the ten sins away from my forty commandments, I'll still be ahead by thirty commandments!" The system does not work that way because the value of the commandments is simply too huge to be wasted on the nullification of a sin, no matter how grave. Put another way: the damage done by a negative, finite act is punished in a similarly finite manner. The value of a positive, finite act, on the other hand, may receive an infinite reward. The Eighth Level thus dictates that the impact of a positive deed rises up without limit to remain in the very presence of God, a place where no negative deed may appear—God "subdues" the transgression, refusing to allow it access to that holy place.

The reason that the consequences of transgression cannot affect the reward for performing commandments is because their origins lie in disparate worlds, as Rabbi Epstein paraphrases Rabbi Cordovero's commentary on the *Zohar*. The commandments were dictated from the highest world of *atsilut*, contracting as they descended through the ten *sefirot* to the lowest world of *asiyah* where they could be performed by human beings. The powers that motivate transgression, on the other hand, emanate from the world of *beriyah* (as per Isaiah 45:7, *u-vorei ra*). The energies released by human actions ultimately return to their heavenly sources: those related to the performance of commandments rise up to *atsilut*, but the energies released by transgressions must stop at *beriyah*. The border between those worlds acts as a barrier, preserving the memory and potency of whatever good humans perform on earth.

Subduing the transgression does not mean eliminating it, as the Midrash states (*Bereshit Rabah* 67:7) in paraphrase: God is patient, but collects what is due. Transgressions must be atoned for in one way or another (see the Second Level for more details). The Eighth Level means God will demand that the transgressions be addressed but will not allow those transgressions to color the fundamentally positive regard God has for the human being.

By way of a very approximate analogy, let us say that someone does a small but significant good deed for the President of the United States. Imagine, for example, that the elderly aunt of the President comes to some official event but is somehow separated from the presidential retinue and is lost, perhaps a little disoriented. Reuven approaches her and asks if he can help, and she explains the situation. Reuven stays with her and uses his cell phone to call the White House, which in turn contacts the Secret Service, and the elderly aunt is rescued. After the event, the President contacts Reuven and thanks him profusely. Getting into the limousine with his Secret Security agents, the President pauses and says, "anytime you need something—give me a call." With that, the President enters the car and it speeds away.

Three weeks later Reuven contacts the White House and asks to speak to the President. The Chief of Staff, who is aware of the President's promise, allows the call to go through to the Oval Office. The President smiles as he picks up the telephone, saying "Reuven, I'm glad you called." Reuven clears his throat and says, "Mr. President, I wanted to take you up on your kind offer and ask you to help me with something."

"It would be my pleasure, Reuven. What is the situation?"

"Well, Mr. President, the other day I went to the dentist, and when I came back to my car, there was this parking ticket on my windshield. It will cost me $18 dollars. I was hoping you could, you know, take care of it."

"Pardon?"

"Have it cancelled, you know, so I don't have to pay $18."

There is a moment of silence, and the President replies, "Reuven, I'm sorry, you'll have to deal with that one on your own. Please call me back when you have something really important to ask. I hate to cut this call short, but I have several world leaders in the office right now, and have to get back to our meeting." He hangs up.

The President's refusal to help is a kind of "subduing of transgression," similar to the Eighth Level. The value of a single favor from the most politically powerful person in the world is huge! Why would someone squander it on something as minor as a parking ticket? What a waste to use that massive opportunity on such a trifle! Reuven should pay the fine associated with the ticket, and leave his credit with the President intact until he really needs it. At the time, Reuven would have preferred that his credit for rescuing the elderly aunt be leveraged to wipe out the traffic ticket, but the President did not agree. He subdued the transgression and did not allow it to rise up to a level of significance equal to the reward commensurate with Reuven's consideration for the Presidential aunt. Reuven was left with an $18 bill but his reward remained intact.

In such a manner, God does not accept a "bribe," to use the biblical term. God grants us immensely huge rewards for all our good deeds, cherishing them and keeping them close by. When a transgression appears, God acknowledges it but refuses to allow it to enter that same central space, casting it back down and thereby preserving the pristine respect and affection that God has for the person. He will not sacrifice a single one of the good deeds for something as small as a transgression. From the human perspective, this means that we are responsible for our actions in the mundane world and must deal with the consequences of sin, yet we know that our merits are preserved and maintained with the utmost security.

God maintains a core of forgiveness for every human being, a place where only the good a person does is recorded and remembered. God is certainly not ignorant of human failings; rather, God refuses to grant these weaknesses with the same degree of significance that the strengths receive. The message for us is clear: we must similarly create a core of forgiveness for those around us, remembering their positive deeds and refusing to taint these memories with their misdeeds. The Eighth Level of Mercy represents an extremely potent tool for forgiveness, especially relevant for family. Rabbi Cordovero urges us to develop a sacred core of forgiveness for our spouses, our parents, our siblings and children, and return to that core whenever challenged by the inevitable minor conflicts that affect daily family life. The phrase "what have you done for me lately?" should never enter the family dynamic; rather, we should develop and preserve a safe space in our hearts for all our loved ones, a place where all their positive deeds and attributes are remembered and shielded from the impact of more recent failings.

Practical Applications

"I hate you!" Irit holds her elbows straight to her sides, fists clenched as she stamps. "You're ruining my life! You never let me do anything I want!"

"You can hang out with your friends at the mall another day. Today," says Emunah, her mother, "you really have to come with the rest of us to visit your grandmother in the nursing home."

"I hate you! You don't understand me at all! You're the worst mother ever! All my friends say so!"

She's still a child. No matter what she says, Emunah maintains a core of love for Irit, and nothing can change that. Emunah remembers the Eighth Level.

If there's one thing Mordechai can't stand, it's when the kids mess around with his computer. Somehow, it's happened again—his screen resolution has been changed, a pile of games have been downloaded to the desktop, and who knows what kind of damage has been done to his files! Fuming, he sits down and logs in to set everything back to normal, congratulating himself for never giving administrator privileges to the kids. Only he knows the administrator password, and therefore they can never really do any permanent damage. As the only administrator on this computer, he can always return the computer to a restore point that eliminates whatever mess the kids left behind.

As he works his way through the process, Mordechai recalls the Eighth Level of Mercy and realizes the parallel to his situation. Sure, the kids were mischievous, but their impact is limited because they don't have administrator privileges on the computer. Denied access to the highest level of authority, whatever wrong they did can be undone with just a few keystrokes. God, as the ultimate Administrator, also refuses to allow harm to enter the highest world of *atsilut* and subduing transgression in the world of *beriyah*. Mordechai realizes that he can apply the Eighth Level to his children at the computer terminal and beyond. He calms down as he contemplates how much he loves his children, a love that cannot be affected by their misbehavior.

The Ninth Level: Bury the Past

Introduction

The Ninth Level of Mercy addresses a principle common to both Kabbalah and modern physics: energy never dissipates of its own accord; rather it is redirected and absorbed into something else. If a stone is dropped into the middle of a still lake, the ripples will extend to the shoreline, their amplitude gradually decreasing in size as the circle of their impact increases. Once they reach the land, the energy represented by the ripples is transferred to the earth itself, shifting the pebbles and grains of sand until the force of the original stone is completely exhausted. The same phenomenon is true of human sin. Sin releases the forces of judgment into the world like a stone dropping into a lake, and the energy of these forces of judgment can only be redirected and absorbed elsewhere. It will not simply stop and return to its source.

The Ninth Level acknowledges God's mercy as it is expressed in the redirection of these forces of judgment. Rabbi Cordovero illustrates the phenomenon with several Biblical examples, including the punishment of Pharaoh (Exodus 4:21), the scapegoat (Leviticus 16), and Daniel's interpretation of the dream of Nebuchadnezzar (Daniel 2). The Ninth Level concludes with a treatment of how we may internalize and emulate this aspect of mercy in our own lives.

התשיעית - וְתַשְׁלִיךְ בִּמְצֻלוֹת יָם כָּל חַטֹּאותָם

זוֹ מִדָּה טוֹבָה לְהַבָּ"ה שֶׁהֲרֵי יִשְׂרָאֵל חָטְאוּ מְסָרָם בְּיַד פַּרְעֹה וְשָׁבוּ בִּתְשׁוּבָה לָמָּה יַעֲנִישׁ פַּרְעֹה וְכֵן סַנְחֵרִיב וְכֵן הָמָן וְדוֹמֵיהֶם אֵין הַבָּ"ה מִתְנַחֵם לוֹמַר שָׁבוּ בִּתְשׁוּבָה אִם כֵּן לֹא יִהְיֶה לָהֶם עוֹד רָעָה אִם כֵּן יִסְתַּלֵּק הָמָן מֵעֲלֵיהֶם אוֹ פַּרְעֹה אוֹ סַנְחֵרִיב זֶה לֹא יַסְפִּיק אֶלָּא יָשׁוּב עֲמַל הָמָן עַל רֹאשׁוֹ וְכֵן פַּרְעֹה וְכֵן סַנְחֵרִיב וְהַטַּעַם לְהַנְהָגָה זוֹ הִיא בְּסוֹד וְנָשָׂא הַשָּׂעִיר עָלָיו אֶת כָּל עֲוֹנֹתָם אֶל אֶרֶץ גְּזֵרָה וּפֵרוּשׁוֹ שֶׁהַשָּׂעִיר נוֹשֵׂא עֲווֹנוֹת מַמָּשׁ, וְזֶה קָשֶׁה מְאֹד וְכִי יִשְׂרָאֵל חָטְאוּ וְהַשָּׂעִיר נוֹשֵׂא. אֶלָּא הַמִּדָּה הִיא כָּךְ הָאָדָם מִתְוַדֶּה וְכַוָּנָתוֹ בַּוִּדּוּי לְקַבֵּל עָלָיו טָהֳרָה כְּעִנְיָן שֶׁאָמַר דָּוִד הֶרֶב כַּבְּסֵנִי מֵעֲוֹנִי וְכֵן הוּא אָמְרֵנוּ מַחוֹק בְּרַחֲמֶיךָ הָרַבִּים אֵינוֹ מִתְפַּלֵּל אֶלָּא שֶׁיִּהְיוּ יִסּוּרִים קַלִּים שֶׁלֹּא יִהְיֶה בָּהֶם בִּטּוּל תּוֹרָה. וְזֶה שֶׁאוֹמְרִים אֲבָל לֹא עַל יְדֵי יִסּוּרִים רָעִים וְכָךְ הוּא מְכֻוָּן בִּהְיוֹתוֹ אוֹמֵר וְאַתָּה צַדִּיק עַל כָּל הַבָּא עָלַי מַמָּשׁ הוּא מְקַבֵּל יִסּוּרִים בְּסֵבֶר פָּנִים יָפוֹת לְהִתְכַּפֵּר מִפְּנֵי שֶׁיֵּשׁ עֲווֹנוֹת שֶׁיִּסּוּרִים מְמָרְקִים אוֹ מִיתָה מְמָרֶקֶת. וְכָךְ הִיא הַמִּדָּה מִיָּד מִתְוַדֶּה בִּתְפִלָּתוֹ וּפֵרְשׁוּ בַּזֹּהַר פָּרָשַׁת פְּקוּדֵי שֶׁהוּא חֵלֶק סָמָאֵל כְּעֵין הַשָּׂעִיר, מַהוּ חֶלְקוֹ שֶׁהַבָּ"ה גּוֹזֵר עָלָיו יִסּוּרִים וּמִיָּד מִזְדַּמֵּן שָׁם סָמָאֵל וְהוֹלֵךְ וְגוֹבֶה

חוֹבוֹ וַהֲרֵי נוֹשֵׂא הַשָּׂעִיר הָעֲוֹנוֹת שֶׁהֲב"ה נוֹתֵן לוֹ רְשׁוּת לִגְבּוֹת חוֹבוֹ וְיִשְׂרָאֵל מִתְטַהֲרִים וְהִנֵּה הַכֹּל יִתְגַּלְגֵּל עַל סָמָאֵל, וְהַטַּעַם שֶׁהֲב"ה גּוֹזֵר עַל עוֹלָמוֹ שֶׁכָּל מִי שֶׁיַּעֲשֶׂה כֵן יִתְבַּטֵּל, וְזֶה טַעַם וְאֶת הַבְּהֵמָה תַּהֲרֹגוּ וְכֵן הָאֶבֶן שֶׁל מִצְוַת הַנִּסְקָלִין וְהַסַּיִף שֶׁל מִצְוַת הַנֶּהֱרָגִין טְעוּנִין קְבוּרָה לְבַטֵּל מְצִיאוּתָם וְכֹחָם אַחַר שֶׁנִּגְמַר דִּינָם. וַהֲרֵי בָזֶה מַמָּשׁ סוֹד הַצֶּלֶם שֶׁל נְבוּכַדְנֶאצַּר נִמְסְרוּ יִשְׂרָאֵל בְּיַד מֶלֶךְ בָּבֶל רֵישָׁא דִּי דַהֲבָא דִכְנֶגֶד הַהוּא רֵישָׁא נִמְסְרוּ בְּיַד פָּרַס שֶׁהֵן חֲדוֹהִי וּדְרָעוֹהִי דִי כְסַף וְכֵן נִדְחוּ אֵלּוּ מִפְּנֵי אֵלּוּ עַד שֶׁיָּרְדוּ יִשְׂרָאֵל לְרַגְלוֹהִי מִנְהֵן דִּי פַרְזֶל וּמִנְהֵן דִּי חֲסַף שֶׁמָּא יִהְיֶה תַּכְלִית הַכֹּל בְּסוֹף הב"ה מַעֲמִידָם וְעוֹשֶׂה בָּהֶם דִּין כְּדִכְתִיב חֲצִי אֲכַלָּה בָּם חֲצִי כָלִים וְיִשְׂרָאֵל אֵינָם כָלִים בֵּאדַיִן דָּקוּ כַחֲדָא דַהֲבָא כַּסְפָּא וּנְחָשָׁא וְכוּ' הִנֵּה בַּהַתְחָלָה כְּתִיב וּמְחָת לְצַלְמָא עַל רַגְלוֹהִי אֵין מִכָּל הַצֶּלֶם אֶלָּא רַגְלָיו שֶׁכְּבָר נִתְבַּטֵּל כֹּחָם וְעָבְרוּ רֹאשׁ וּדְרָעוֹהִי וּמְעוֹהִי וְעִם כָּל זֶה בַּסּוֹף דָּקוּ כַּחֲדָא, עָתִיד הב"ה לְהַעֲמִיד סָמָאֵל וְהָרְשָׁעִים שֶׁעָשׂוּ מַעֲשָׂיו וּפְעֻלּוֹתָיו וְיַעֲשֶׂה בָּהֶם הַדִּין. וְהִנּוּ וְתַשְׁלִיךְ בִּמְצֻלוֹת יָם כָּל חַטֹּאותָם.

יֵרָצֶה מַשְׁלִיךְ כֹּחַ הַדִּין לְהִפָּעֵל עַל יְדֵי אֵלּוּ שֶׁהֵם מְצוּלוֹת יָם וְהָרְשָׁעִים כַּיָּם נִגְרָשׁ כִּי הַשְׁקֵט לֹא

יוּכָל וַיְגָרְשׁוּ מֵימָיו רֶפֶשׁ וָטִיט אֵלּוּ הֵם הָעוֹשִׂים דִּין בְּיִשְׂרָאֵל שֶׁיָּשׁוּב אַחַר כָּל גְּמוּלָם בְּרֹאשָׁם.

וְהַטַּעַם מִפְּנֵי שֶׁאַחַר שֶׁיִּשְׂרָאֵל קִבְּלוּ הַדִּין הב"ה מִתְנַחֵם אֲפִלּוּ עַל מַה שֶּׁקָּדַם וְתוֹבֵעַ עֶלְבּוֹנָם וְלֹא דַי אֶלָּא אֲנִי קָצַפְתִּי מְעַט וְהֵמָּה עָזְרוּ לְרָעָה.

גַּם בְּמִדָּה זוֹ צָרִיךְ לְהִתְנַהֵג הָאָדָם עִם חֲבֵרוֹ, אֲפִלּוּ שֶׁיִּהְיֶה רָשָׁע מְדֻכָּא בְּיִסּוּרִין אַל יִשְׂנָאֵהוּ שֶׁאַחַר שֶׁנִּקְלָה הֲרֵי הוּא כְּאָחִיךָ וִיקָרֵב הַמְּרוּדִים וְהַנֶּעֱנָשִׁים וִירַחֵם עֲלֵיהֶם וְאַדְּרַבָּה יַצִּילֵם מִיַּד אוֹיֵב וְאַל יֹאמַר עֲווֹנוֹ גָּרַם לוֹ אֶלָּא יְרַחֲמֵהוּ בְּמִדָּה זוֹ כִּדְפֵרַשְׁתִּי:

The Ninth Level

And cast all their sins into the depths of the sea

God expresses goodness in this Level. When the Jewish people sinned, God handed them over to Pharaoh. Why was Pharaoh punished when the Jews repented? The same question may be asked of Sennacherib, and Haman, and their ilk. God does not say, "the Jews repented, and therefore no more evil will befall them," and simply removing the threat of Haman, or Pharaoh, or Sennacherib. This is not enough. Instead, God causes Haman's plans to redound upon his own head, and so too Pharaoh, and so too Sennacherib. The principle is based on the secret of *and the goat will bear upon itself all their sins to the land of Gezerah.* The goat literally bears the sins, a very difficult concept. Should the goat be held responsible for the sin of the Jewish people? Yes, as follows: when a person confesses, the confession is uttered with the intention of attaining purity, as David said "wash me, cleanse me of my sins," and we say, "erase in Your great mercy." We pray that our punishments be light, and not cause us to neglect the study of Torah. This is the significance of the continuation of that prayer, "but not through difficult tribulations," and the intent behind the concluding phrase, "and You are righteous regarding all that happens to me." There are sins that are nullified by tribulations, while others are nullified by death, and thus one cheerfully accepts atonement through tribulations. As soon as one confesses in prayer, the confession becomes the goat, the portion of Samael, as the Zohar explains in *Parashat Pekudei*. What is this portion? God visits punishments upon the person, and Samael immediately appears to collect his debt. Samael received permission from God to collect, but the transgression has devolved onto the goat, and thus the Jewish people are purified while Samael receives his due. Ultimately, God's decree was that anyone who performed this service in the world would be nullified, which is the meaning of *and you will kill the animal*. Similarly the rock used for stoning and the sword used for execution both require burial in order to eliminate both their existence and power after the sentence has been performed. This is precisely the secret of the Nebuchadnezzar's statue. The Jews were handed over to the King of Babylon, *the head of gold*. When this head was bowed, they were handed over to Persia, *a chest and arms of gold*, which was ultimately replaced, until the Jews arrived at *the legs of bronze and feet of clay*. What will be the final, positive end? God will force them to rise and face justice, as it is written: *I will expend My arrows on them*. My arrows will destroy, but the Jewish people will not be destroyed. *The pieces of iron, clay, brass, silver and gold will be destroyed*. The verse begins, *and he struck the image to its legs*, meaning that the only parts left of the image were the legs, because their power had already been nullified by the destruction of the head, arms and chest. Nevertheless, at the end it is written *they will be destroyed as one*, meaning that in the future God will force even Samael to stand up along with the wicked people who carry out his various deeds, and God will judge them.

This is the meaning of *and cast all their sins into the depths of the sea*, meaning God will send the power of justice to bring down all those who are like the depths of the sea—*the wicked are like a stormy sea, it cannot be silent and its waters churn up silt and mud*. The verse refers to those who execute judgment upon the Jewish people. God will ultimately cause their actions to redound to their own heads.

Once the Jewish people accept their punishment, God reconsiders even what came before. God demands retribution for the sake of their dignity. Moreover, God says *I was but a little angered, but they compounded the evil*.

One must employ this Level when dealing with others. Even if a wicked person is afflicted by punishments, one should not hate him, for after he is lashed he is like your brother. One should draw close those who rebelled and those who were punished, and have mercy upon them. One should save them from an enemy, and not say, "his sin caused this to happen." Rather, one should show him mercy with this Level, as I have explained.

Commentary

Rabbi Cordovero delves into the deeper kabbalistic understanding of the mechanics of repentance in this Level. When a person commits a transgression, this creates a type of energy debt that must, at some point, be collected. God sends the angel Samael to demand payment, and as described in Levels 1 and 2, the price can be exceptionally dear: Samael is also known as the Angel of Death. If, however, the sinner repents, he or she is exempted from payment of the full debt, as the energy expended in the difficult process of repentance is accepted by God as sufficient to cover the immediate responsibility for the transgression, even though a large balance remains. God, in other words, will accept the lower payoff price of confession and repentance, but the Divine balance sheet must still be reconciled: what happens to the remainder of the debt of sin? Samael and his collectors may not return empty-handed. Once they are loosed upon the world, they discharge their terrible duties in full.

Ironically, the Talmud expresses a certain degree of grudging sympathy for Samael, for his task is nearly impossible. "Break the barrel," God commands Samael, "but save the wine" (*Bava Batra* 16a), meaning, push the people to their absolute limits, but do not destroy them. Samael is duty-bound to collect, but he may not overreach by commanding more than a person is able to provide. Rabbi Epstein cites a memorable parable from *Sefer Me'irat Einayim:* Samael is like a dog begging for scraps at his master's table. So long as the dog is ignored, he will not leave his master's side. Once the master gives him a bone, the dog retreats to a corner and happily chews on his prize, leaving the master to enjoy his meal in peace. The bone is only a fraction of the meal as a whole, providing little caloric energy, but the dog will be satisfied with this token.

Similarly, Samael is prepared to accept a small concession, a sacrifice prepared under particular conditions, and consider the debt paid in full. The necessary conditions for this sacrifice are covered in the process of *teshuvah*.

In the Third Level of Mercy ("Take Care of it Personally"), Rabbi Cordovero cites Isaiah 4:4 to describe how God washes away the filth of the daughters of Zion as the final stage of the process of *teshuvah*. Here in the Ninth Level, Rabbi Cordovero adds a citation from Psalm 51 to emphasize the cleansing power of repentance. The water metaphor is especially significant in the context of the debt due to Samael and his legions: the rinse water, soiled with the filth of human sin, is accepted as payment of the debt of sin (*Tefilah Le-Moshe* 6:6). In other words, the byproduct of repentance, the water sloughed off a soul as it is purified through contrition, serves the purpose of appeasing those forces sent to exact retribution for sin. No energy is wasted in this ecosystem: even the discarded water has its purpose. The instruments of change, whether understood as the cleansing properties of water or the coercive potential of punishment, are directed to Samael once their function has been discharged.

Rabbi Cordovero offers several examples to reinforce the counterintuitive yet salvific power of punishment for the catalysts that engender human change. Pharaoh, for example, could not merely return to his palace and remain undisturbed after Exodus from Egypt: his punishment represented the final expiation necessary for the redemption of the Jewish people. His hateful persecution of the Jews, expressed first through his own will and later reinforced as God hardened his heart, served to effect massive *teshuvah* among the enslaved Jews. Pharaoh's influence over the Jews was immediately removed, like the water that rinses off the daughters of Zion. Just as that water is directed to Samael as payment for his original charge, so too was Pharaoh punished for his crimes. Pharaoh acted as the emissary of Samael, and must perforce return to his master once his function was fulfilled. This is also the meaning of Nebuchadnezzar's dream, as interpreted by the prophet Daniel. All the various nations that persecuted the Jewish people, expressed in the dream as an effigy made of gold, silver, bronze and clay, will ultimately be punished even when they no longer have any power over the Jews.

The phenomenon of punishment for those who punish even extends to non-human and even inanimate objects. If an ox gores a person to death, under certain circumstances Jewish law requires that the ox be put to death. During the Temple era, should the Sanhedrin issue a death sentence, the sword that was used to carry out the punishment was buried after the execution. The Ninth Level is also operational in the entire sacrificial process, as Rabbi Cordovero illustrates with the pithy comment, "should the goat be held responsible for the sins of the Jewish people?" This is a reference to the Yom Kippur service, which in ancient times involved the sacrifice of a goat that bore the sins of the Jewish people (the "scapegoat"). The goat did nothing wrong at all, but when the Jewish people are sincerely repentant, God invokes the Ninth Level, "casting their sins into the depths of the sea," or in this case onto the goat, and the animal is sacrificed in their place.

Rabbi Cordovero's description of the Ninth Level of Mercy provides a Kabbalistic understanding of the process of *teshuvah*, most of which occurs on the metaphysical level. On the human level, we have little to do with the disposal of the rise water and the fulfillment of the debt to Samael, functions that are discharged without our awareness. At the same time, *Date of Devorah* is dedicated to the practice of *imitatio Dei*, and therefore Rabbi Cordovero outlines ways in which we can participate even in this Level of Mercy.

The Torah prescribes corporal punishment, specifically lashes, for particular crimes. The Midrash *Sifri* notes that the Torah has an unusual turn of phrase regarding lashes. Deuteronomy 25:3 reads, *forty stripes may be given him, but no more…lest your brother be degraded in your eyes*. The ancient sage Rabbi Hananyah ben Gamliel comments, "all day [the criminal] was called 'wicked'…yet once he has received his lashes, the Torah calls him *your brother*." In other words, once the punishment has been imposed, the sinner must be readmitted completely to the fold as "your brother." Cleansed of his sin, the discarded waste water fulfills all debts. Rabbi Cordovero concludes the Ninth Level of Mercy with the directive that we should recognize this in our own interactions with those who have completed their repentance: accept them fully as our siblings and move on.

Sometimes, human conflict inheres in an inanimate object: an article of clothing, an empty bottle, a receipt. The Ninth Level of Mercy presents a strategy for resolving lingering conflict through the ritual destruction of that object. Like the executioner's sword, the object must be buried after it has discharged its function. Do not simply dispose of the object like trash, realize that it represents the rinse water of *teshuvah*, the cleansing process that will restore the relationship to its prior health. The object may also be the bone thrown to the dogs to divert their attention from the meal, and removing it from your home will eliminate a painful reminder of earlier conflict.

Practical Applications

It was stupid, and Asher really should have known better. Did he really think that she would appreciate that joke birthday card that emphasized Shoshana's age? He knew it from the look on her face when she took it out of the envelope. She managed to maintain a smile for everyone else at the table, but was he really surprised that she didn't take it with her when she left the party?

Asher understands he should not return the card to Shoshana. He gives it one last look, and commits to memory the pain he caused her. He resolves to make it up to her, and invokes the Ninth Level by throwing the birthday card away.

Naftali has difficulty forgiving himself for his heavy drinking. It's in his past, but he can't get over the things he said and did while under the influence of alcohol. He knows there is is value in remembering his misdeeds, but he is often paralyzed by his remorse. He needs to manage his regret so that he may become spiritually free to improve himself.

Naftali decides to divert some of his remorse onto an inanimate object. First, he writes out his regrets, longhand on paper, and tucks this document into an envelope. Then, he enlists the help of Gad, a trusted friend who will make sure he carries through on his intent. Gad buys him a bottle of the vodka Naftali once favored, and together they pour the alcohol down the kitchen sink. Naftali rolls up the envelope and places it in the bottle, along with a few symbolic items that remind him of his past misdeeds: a cigarette, a printout of an email from his former boss, an eyeliner that Devorah once left in his car. Naftali and Gad then take the bottle, fill it with pebbles and dirt from the back yard, and drive out to the bridge. Standing at the pinnacle of the bridge, Naftali utters a brief, heartfelt prayer for forgiveness, and releases his past, which sinks to the bottom of the river even as his prayers rise upward.

The Tenth Level: Do the Right Thing Anyway

Introduction

The Tenth, Eleventh and Twelfth Levels together comprise a triad of strategies for forgiving others, particularly people with whom we have more casual relationships. The Tenth Level addresses the average person, with neither elevated nor stunted morality, the Eleventh Level describes forgiveness for the person who habitually goes beyond the minimum requirements to help others, and the Twelfth Level focuses on forgiving people who typically fall short of our moral expectations.

The Tenth and Eleventh Levels are also associated with the Patriarchs Jacob and Abraham, respectively. Jacob, whose tribulations frequently involved suffering at the hands of cruel and deceitful individuals like his brother Esau and his father-in-law Laban, learned strategies for coping with challenging people without sacrificing his fundamental trait of Truth. The Tenth Level therefore addresses this issue of truth in forgiveness, and just as Jacob's deception of Isaac is understood as appropriate despite its manipulation of apparent truth, so too does forgiveness require a slight but intentional deviation from the apparently just. Simply put, even though an individual might deserve a strict retribution for a hurtful act, nevertheless one should just ease that response slightly in favor of mercy, tempering judgment with kindness even though the situation may not otherwise warrant a forgiving response.

הָעֲשִׂירִית - תִּתֵּן אֱמֶת לְיַעֲקֹב

מִדָּה זוֹ הִיא, שֶׁיֵּשׁ לְיִשְׂרָאֵל מַעֲלַת אֹתָם הַבֵּינוֹנִיִּים שֶׁאֵינָם יוֹדְעִים לְהִתְנַהֵג לִפְנִים מִשּׁוּרַת הַדִּין וְהֵם נִקְרָאִים יַעֲקֹב מִפְּנֵי שֶׁאֵינָם מִתְנַהֲגִים אֶלָּא עִם הַנְהָגָה אֲמִתִּית.

גַּם הַבָּ"ה יֵשׁ לוֹ מִדַּת אֱמֶת שֶׁהִיא עַל צַד מְצִיאוּת הַמִּשְׁפָּט הַיָּשָׁר, וְאֵלּוּ הֵם הַמִּתְנַהֲגִים בָּעוֹלָם בְּיֹשֶׁר וְהַבָּ"ה מִתְנַהֵג עִמָּהֶם בֶּאֱמֶת מְרַחֵם עֲלֵיהֶם עַל צַד הַיֹּשֶׁר וְהַמִּשְׁפָּט.

גַּם כֵּן הָאָדָם צָרִיךְ לְהִתְנַהֵג עִם חֲבֵרוֹ עַל צַד הַיֹּשֶׁר וְהָאֱמֶת בְּלִי לְהַטּוֹת מִשְׁפַּט חֲבֵרוֹ אֶלָּא לְרַחֵם עָלָיו בֶּאֱמֶת כְּמוֹ שֶׁהַבָּ"ה מְרַחֵם עַל הַבְּרִיּוֹת הַבֵּינוֹנִיּוֹת בְּמִדַּת אֱמֶת לְתַקֵּן אֹתָם:

The Tenth Level

Give Truth to Jacob

This Level refers to those members of the Jewish people who have a certain quality: they are intermediates, meaning they do not know how to behave beyond the letter of the law. Such people are called "Jacob." This is because they only behave according to principles which are demonstrably true.

God also has this trait of truth, which refers to that which is apparently just and upright. Those people who behave in this world in a correct fashion are treated by God with truth. God shows them mercy out of justice and righteousness.

So too should a person behave with others, justly and with righteousness, without perverting judgment. One should show another mercy in truth, just as God shows mercy to the average creature with the Level of truth, to address their imperfections.

Commentary

Kabbalistic thought ascribes the quality of truth to the patriarch Jacob. Cursory readers of the Bible may find this surprising. Jacob, at his mother's insistence, impersonated his brother Esau to deceive their father Isaac into giving Jacob the blessing of the first-born. Jacob, in reaction to the sharp business practices of his father-in-law Laban, manipulated the behavior of Laban's sheep to ensure that Jacob would receive a larger inheritance. How can Jacob be associated with the attribute of Truth?

The answer lies in the attributes associated most prominently with his father and grandfather. Abraham, the grandfather, was known for his overwhelming kindness (*hesed*), seeking to host travelers even while he recovered from his self-circumcision at age 99. Isaac, the father, was known for his incredible self-control (*gevurah*), submitting himself as willing sacrifice at age 37. Jacob, the son, represents a blending and balancing of these two characteristics, finding the glorious space (*tiferet*) between the two. Represented graphically in the *sefirot*, Jacob's trait of *tiferet* sits below *hesed* and *gevurah*, equidistant between the two.

Rabbi Cordovero's understanding of the attribute of Truth includes another element. Truth is not simply the perfect balance of kindness and self-restraint. Truth requires a slight shifting of that balance toward kindness, a subtle tendency toward the right which is expressed in Hebrew as *lifnim mi-shurat ha-din*, or "beyond the letter of the law." For Rabbi Cordovero, acting with Truth means giving others a measure of kindness beyond what they deserve.

Rabbi Aharon David Goldberg illuminates another strange aspect of the naming of this Level in his commentary on *Date Palm of Devorah*. Should Jacob, one of the Patriarchs of the Jewish people, be compared to an intermediate who does not know how to behave beyond the letter of the law? Jacob, who endured the trickery of his father-in-law Laban to the extent that he spent fourteen years working to marry his beloved Rachel? Should Jacob be called an average creature? Rabbi Goldberg clarifies that the name Jacob is used here in two senses.

On one level, "Jacob" refers to a type of person, one of the common folk who does not spend much energy on spiritual growth. He may be a very good person, with excellent potential, but the demands of daily life can be overwhelming, particularly given the stresses of earning a living and maintaining a home. He may be so concerned by economic pressures that he has little time or mental resources to spend in contemplation of ethical ideals. To underscore the forbearance such people deserve, Rabbi Goldberg refers to the verse in the Torah that describes the *house of Jacob* (Exodus 19:3) in the context of Rashi's comment there: "speak to them gently."

The type of person described as Jacob is occupied principally by self-interest. This is especially evident when Jacob deals with strangers, because they are furthest away from his own immediate concerns. Jacob has no problem being rude, cutting in line, and generally treating others aggressively in order to get an advantage, however slight. Often, this behavior is deeply counterproductive—Jacob will weave in and out of traffic, placing himself and others at risk, in order to get to his destination a few minutes earlier, yet a small miscalculation can result in a traffic citation or worse, an accident. His rush results in a great delay.

The other sense of Jacob in this Level is in reference to the Patriarch himself. As Rabbi Goldberg continues, Jacob was the Patriarch with the most extensive experience dealing with the crude, cruel outside world. Abraham and Isaac both had extremely difficult lives, not to mention the challenges of raising difficult children, but by comparison with Jacob, these experiences were episodic in nature. Jacob lived for many years in the employ of his crafty father-in-law Laban, the very personification of the individual obsessed with self-interest, even at the expense of his own daughters. Jacob, more than his father and grandfather, needed to develop the skills necessary to work with such individuals. Thus the Tenth Level is correctly named "give truth to Jacob," meaning, give Jacob the strategy of forgiveness appropriate for the challenge of dealing with common people.

Expressed in the Divine context, the Tenth Level refers to God's allowance of an extra measure of mercy even for the common person who fails to extend such generosity to others. The Tenth Level is called Truth because God's mercy nevertheless retains its mathematically precise nature even when it appears to distort judgment to kindness. For example, if Reuven were to steal a hundred dollars from Shimon, it would appear correct that Reuven must return the exact amount of money immediately and in full to Shimon. At the same time, a deeper evaluation of the situation may reveal that Reuven stole the money out of desperation to feed his hungry family, and that he fully intended to repay the debt once he had the wherewithal, and so on. Influenced by such circumstances, a human judge may build some leniencies into the decision rendered against Reuven: he may be granted the ability to repay the debt in small installments rather than all at once, or the debt may be reduced to an amount he can manage, given that Shimon is a wealthy man who hardly noticed the loss of a hundred dollars. Every crime requires a punishment, but Truth requires a judgment that goes beyond the letter of the law. God renders this judgment of Truth to human beings, allowing us time to do *teshuvah* to rectify our misdeeds, considering our suffering in the calculation of our repayment, and thousands of other kindnesses.

Expressed in a human context, the Tenth Level itself is simple: do the right thing anyway. When confronted with a person who strives to take unfair advantage, you may certainly protect yourself from harm, but maintain your ethical balance. Let the small things go. Demonstrate through your actions the immediacy of forgiveness. Daily life involves so many minor acts of cruelty, words and deeds that are by their definition unnecessary: a rude receptionist at the doctor's office, a harsh remark at the shopping mall, a coworker who fails to return a greeting. The Tenth Level acknowledges that a mean response in kind might be justified on one level, but we are required to go beyond the letter of the law and give uncouth people a measure of kindness beyond reciprocity. We cannot control how others will behave, but *Date Palm of Devorah* urges us to control how we respond.

Practical Applications

The traffic is intense, waves of heat shimmering off the hoods of cars locked in for blocks on the highway. Shlomo is only half a mile away from his exit, and then he can get onto the side streets and make his way home for dinner. A honk from a horn to his right draws his attention, and he sees a teenager driving a bright yellow sports car pushing his way into his lane. Irritated, Shlomo is tempted to ignore the young man, pulling up close to the car in front to create an impenetrable barrier to the impudent interloper, but Shlomo has been reading *Date Palm of Devorah*, and he remembers the Tenth Level of Forgiveness. He decides to "do the right thing anyway" and give the driver a break. The extra minute or two added to his evening commute is certainly not as important as treating another person with an extra measure of humanity.

Just as the elevator doors are closing, Shulamit hears someone's rushed footfalls approaching. Before she began learning *Date Palm of Devorah*, she would have stared at her mobile phone with intensity, willing the doors to close before anyone else to get on. Thinking of the Tenth Level, though, Shulamit now reaches for the "door open" button and allows the grateful latecomer to share a ride upward.

The Eleventh Level

Do More for Those Who Do More

Introduction

People build up spiritual credit for helping others, yet they are still human, full of personal imperfections. Recognize the value of their prior kindnesses and give them a little more forgiveness when they err.

הָאַחַת עֶשְׂרֵה - חֶסֶד לְאַבְרָהָם

הֵם הַמִּתְנַהֲגִים בָּעוֹלָם לִפְנִים מִשּׁוּרַת הַדִּין כְּאַבְרָהָם אָבִינוּ גַּם הב"ה מִתְנַהֵג עִמָּהֶם לִפְנִים מִשּׁוּרַת הַדִּין, אֵינוֹ מַעֲמִיד עִמָּהֶם הַדִּין עַל תָּקְפּוֹ אַף לֹא בַּדֶּרֶךְ הַיָּשָׁר אֶלָּא נִכְנָס עִמָּהֶם לִפְנִים מִן הַיֹּשֶׁר כְּמוֹ שֶׁהֵם מִתְנַהֲגִים, וְהַיְנוּ חֶסֶד לְאַבְרָהָם הב"ה מִתְנַהֵג בְּמִדַּת חֶסֶד עִם אוֹתָם שֶׁהֵם כְּמוֹ אַבְרָהָם בְּהִתְנַהֲגוּתָם.

גַּם הָאָדָם עִם הֱיוֹת שֶׁעִם כָּל אָדָם יִהְיֶה מִתְנַהֵג בְּצֶדֶק וּבְיֹשֶׁר וּבְמִשְׁפָּט, עִם הַטּוֹבִים וְהַחֲסִידִים תִּהְיֶה הַנְהָגָתוֹ לִפְנִים מִשּׁוּרַת הַדִּין. וְאִם לִשְׁאָר הָאָדָם הָיָה סַבְלָן קְצָת לְאֵלּוּ יוֹתֵר וְיוֹתֵר, וִירַחֵם עֲלֵיהֶם לְכָנֵס עִמָּהֶם לִפְנִים מִשּׁוּרַת הַדִּין שֶׁהוּא מִתְנַהֵג בָּהּ עִם שְׁאָר הָאָדָם וְצָרִיךְ שֶׁיִּהְיוּ אֵלּוּ חֲשׁוּבִים לְפָנָיו מְאֹד מְאֹד וַחֲבִיבִין לוֹ וְהֵם יִהְיוּ מֵאַנְשֵׁי חֶבְרָתוֹ:

The Eleventh Level

Kindness to Abraham

There are those who behave in this world beyond the letter of the law, like Abraham our father, and God treats them beyond the letter of the law. God does not insist that they suffer the full force of the law, and not even that which would be correct, rather God goes beyond the letter of the law just as these people conduct themselves. This is "kindness to Abraham." God uses the Level of "kindness" with those who are like Abraham in their own behavior.

So too should a person behave. One should always treat others with righteousness, in an upright and just fashion. Nevertheless, with those good and pious people, one should go beyond the letter of the law. If one is a little patient with most people, one should be more patient with these people, showing them mercy beyond the letter of the law, more than one would with other people. One should consider such people exceptionally important and dear, and they should be among one's associates.

Commentary

Abraham the Patriarch (grandfather of Jacob) is associated in Jewish thought with the character trait of *hesed*, or "kindness." The Midrash records, for example, that Abraham was especially hospitable to travelers, an exceptionally valued behavior in the harsh desert climate. He would habitually open his tent on all four sides in order to be certain he would not miss passers-by from any direction. Even when he was recuperating from his circumcision, self-administered at the age of ninety-nine, the Torah describes him sitting by his tent waiting to open his home to strangers. God took pity on him and made the sun especially hot that day, both to aid in Abraham's healing as well as to discourage travelers from bothering him, but when God saw that Abraham was not deterred from his usual course of seeking to help others, God sent three angels so that Abraham could exercise his customary *hesed*.

The Eleventh Level describes how God will be especially merciful with those who have a history of being merciful with others, in accordance with the Talmudic dictum, "as you measure others, so shall you be measured." If a person is spiritually stingy, preferring to concentrate on the faults of others and determining their treatment by recalling their failures, then God will reciprocate by imposing similar standards. On the other hand, a person who is spiritually generous, focusing on the potential of others for goodness, will be judged with a similarly lenient standard. Human good will generates Divine good will.

Rabbi Cordovero therefore urges us to reach within ourselves to extend an extra measure of forgiveness to those who have a history of forgiving others. This should be understood in the larger sense of "forgiveness," meaning, they have a demonstrated pattern of donating of themselves to others, perhaps through sustained charitable work, giving of their own resources to benefit others. This may mean monetary donations, or donations of their own time to volunteer in various capacities for the benefit of the larger community. It certainly includes those people who choose professions that support the weaker elements of society yet are not typically recognized by high salaries—teachers, social workers, and so on. It also includes people who place their own well-being at risk for the benefit of others, such as firemen and policemen, and those who subordinate their own time to the immediate needs of others in emergencies, including first responders such as ambulance drivers.

The Eleventh Level demands that when we see a human failing in these people, we should do our utmost to extend forgiveness to them. As the Talmud teaches, "when you see a learned person sin, do not contemplate it—by the morning he has certainly repented."

Practical Applications

You're driving in your neighborhood one day and happen to notice a casual acquaintance walking on the sidewalk. You know he lives a fair distance away, long enough that he would normally be driving as well. Perhaps his car is being serviced? As you ponder this, you recall how he does a lot of community volunteer work, promoting the local blood drive and things like that. Remembering the Eleventh Level, you decide to "do more for those who do more." You pull over to offer him a lift to his destination.

Who is asking for a favor? It is of course praiseworthy to help anyone in need, but sometimes it's just very difficult to give of your own time or resources for someone else. If you were asked by a casual acquaintance and would politely refuse, think again if that acquaintance is someone who personally donates time, energy or money to other worthy causes. Recognize that this person does valuable things for the larger community, and go beyond your normal limitations to do the favor anyway.

The Twelfth Level

Remember Where They Came From

Introduction

Even after considering the previous eleven strategies, it may be difficult to find a path to forgiveness. The Twelfth Level suggests a shift of focus, from the offender to his or her family background. Even when a Jew behaves inappropriately, and little excuse for the behavior may be found, nevertheless that Jew is still a child of Abraham, Isaac, Jacob, and deserves purely out of respect for the merit of the ancestors.

השתים עשרה - אֲשֶׁר נִשְׁבַּעְתָּ לַאֲבֹתֵינוּ

יֵשׁ בְּנֵי אָדָם שֶׁאֵינָם הֲגוּנִים וְהַקָּבָּ"ה מְרַחֵם עַל כֻּלָּם וּפֵרְשׁוּ בַּגְּמָרָא וַחֲנַתִּי אֶת אֲשֶׁר אָחֹן שֶׁאָמַר הַקָּבָּ"ה אוֹצָר זֶה לְאוֹתָם שֶׁאֵינָם הֲגוּנִים יֵשׁ אוֹצָר תַּחֲנוּנִים שֶׁהַקָּבָּ"ה חוֹנֵן וְנוֹתֵן לָהֶם מַתְּנַת חִנָּם לְפִי שֶׁאָמַר הַקָּבָּ"ה הֲרֵי יֵשׁ לָהֶם זְכוּת אָבוֹת, אֲנִי נִשְׁבַּעְתִּי לָאָבוֹת אִם כֵּן עִם הֱיוֹת שֶׁאֵינָם הֲגוּנִים יִזְכּוּ בִּשְׁבִיל שֶׁהֵם מִזֶּרַע הָאָבוֹת שֶׁנִּשְׁבַּעְתִּי לָהֶם לְפִיכָךְ אַנְהִילֵם וְאַנְהִיגֵם עַד שֶׁיִּתָּקְנוּ. וְכָךְ יִהְיֶה הָאָדָם אַף אִם יִפְגַּע בָּרְשָׁעִים אַל יִתְאַכְזֵר כְּנֶגְדָּם אוֹ יְחָרְפָם וְכַיּוֹצֵא, אֶלָּא יְרַחֵם עֲלֵיהֶם, וְיֹאמַר סוֹף סוֹף הֵם בְּנֵי אַבְרָהָם יִצְחָק וְיַעֲקֹב, אִם הֵם אֵינָם כְּשֵׁרִים, אֲבוֹתֵיהֶם כְּשֵׁרִים וַהֲגוּנִים, וְהַמְבַזֶּה הַבָּנִים מְבַזֶּה הָאָבוֹת, אֵין רְצוֹנִי שֶׁיִּתְבַּזּוּ אֲבוֹתֵיהֶם עַל יָדַי, וּמְכַסֶּה עֶלְבּוֹנָם וּמְתַקְּנָם כְּפִי כֹּחוֹ.

The Twelfth Level

That You Swore to Our Ancestors

There are those people who do not behave correctly, yet God shows mercy to all. The Talmud explains the verse, *I will show kindness to whom I will show kindness*: God says, "I have a storehouse for those who are unworthy." There is a storehouse of kindness, from which God dispenses freely to those who are unworthy, because God says, "behold, they have the merit of their ancestors. I swore to their ancestors!" Thus, even though they are unworthy, they receive merit because they are the descendants of their ancestors, "to whom I swore," therefore I will lead and guide them until they address their imperfections." So too should a human being act. If one encounters wicked people, one should not be cruel to them, insulting them and the like, rather one should show them mercy and say, "in the end, they are the children of Abraham, Isaac and Jacob. Even if they are not proper, their ancestors were proper and good. One who derides the children derides the parents, and I do not wish to be the cause of derision of the ancestors." One should protect their dignity and help them as much as possible.

Commentary

The Twelfth Level relies on a concept known as "the merit of the ancestors." Children inherit the merit earned by previous generations. The inheritance may be eroded by disgraceful conduct, but the children of illustrious generations are born with a kind of a trust fund of merit that serves to protect them from God's anger. This precious store of positive regard should be carefully guarded and developed through further investment in good deeds, and serves as an insurance policy against God's anger. Continuing the financial metaphor, the Twelfth Level is not unlike how we electronically link our savings accounts to our checking accounts. If we ever accidentally go into overdraft in our checking account, the bank will automatically make a transfer from the savings account to cover the deficit.

Another metaphor for the Twelfth Level is the concept of "rollover minutes" promoted by many cell phone providers. The Abramson family is currently on one big Family Plan, with a large number of minutes of talking allowed for the family as a whole. Typically some members of the family talk less than others on the cell phones, and at the end of a given month there's a balance of unused minutes. The cell phone provider kindly sets aside this time as rollover minutes, leaving most of them intact for the following month in case we accidentally speak longer than we expected. The extra time is deducted from the rollover minutes, and we are not charged additional fees for the conversations.

The Jewish people trace their lineage back to three Patriarchs (Abraham, Isaac and Jacob) and four Matriarchs (Sarah, Rebekah, Rachel and Leah), and the merit of these outstandingly righteous people created a massive fund of rollover merit that has been cherished and developed for millennia. When God is disappointed by the behavior of one of their children, God may choose to dip into the ultimate retirement fund and make an automatic transfer, forgiving the offending Jew in the merit of his or her ancestors. God alone can make the determination to process the transfer, as the Torah indicates, "I will show favor to whomsoever I decide." The transfer of merit to cover a deficiency is a type of a gift. God also testifies that this conferring of merit is the result of the promise made to the ancestors. By forgiving otherwise unworthy children, God upholds the covenant made so long ago.

Rabbi Cordovero urges us to adopt a similar strategy. When dealing with a difficult person, one should contemplate their family background. Perhaps this person is unworthy of forgiveness on his or her own merit, but their parents, grandparents, or even earlier ancestors may have done things for others that deserve recognition by later generations. This is especially true with fellow Jews, who can lay claim to the lineage of the Patriarchs Abraham, Isaac and Jacob, and the Matriarchs Sarah, Rebecca, Rachel and Leah. Moreover, when we exercise the Twelfth Level, we even do a "kindness to God," as it were, by forgiving the debt that otherwise would have been paid from the Divine "storehouse of merit." Therefore we should recall the merit of their distant family background, and find cause for forgiveness.

Practical Applications

Reuven has a highly irritating personality that drives you crazy. You would like to have nothing to do with him, but your social circles intersect, and one day you're at a function and you're seated at his table. As he is holding forth on topics and in a manner that you find burdensome, contemplate the fact that Reuven's grandfather was a generous philanthropist who gave much of his wealth to worthwhile projects. Reuven may be a pest, but his grandfather was someone who cared about others deeply. Take a deep breath and tolerate Reuven.

Sarah is a person that, as far as you can tell, has no redeeming characteristics whatsoever. Ideally, you would prefer to write her out of your life altogether, and if you were never to see her again you would have no regrets at all. Nevertheless, she lives right next door, and you are forced to have some sort of interaction with her several times a week. You also remember Sarah's mother, who was a beautiful person who was always ready with a compliment. Whatever Sarah's faults, her mother would certainly be pained if you didn't treat Sarah with tolerance. Give Sarah a break.

The Thirteenth Level

The Moment of Innocence

Introduction

The final Level is an exceptionally powerful tool for forgiveness when all else fails. No matter how far gone a person may be, there was certainly a time when they were completely innocent. Think on that time, and find space for forgiveness.

Level Thirteen

השלוש עשרה - מִימֵי קֶדֶם

הֲרֵי מִדָּה שֶׁיֵּשׁ לְהב"ה עִם יִשְׂרָאֵל כְּשֶׁתַּמָּה זְכוּת וְכַיּוֹצֵא מַה יַּעֲשֶׂה וַהֲרֵי הֵם מִצַּד עַצְמָם אֵינָם הֲגוּנִים, כְּתִ' זָכַרְתִּי לָךְ חֶסֶד נְעוּרַיִךְ אַהֲבַת כְּלוּלֹתָיִךְ.

מַמָּשׁ זוֹכֵר הב"ה יָמִים קַדְמוֹנִים, אַהֲבָה שֶׁהָיָה מִקֹּדֶם וּמְרַחֵם עַל יִשְׂרָאֵל וּבָזֶה יַזְכִּיר לָהֶם כָּל הַמִּצְווֹת שֶׁעָשׂוּ מִיּוֹם שֶׁנּוֹלְדוּ וְכָל הַטּוֹבוֹת וְכָל הַמִּדּוֹת טוֹבוֹת שֶׁהב"ה מַנְהִיג בָּהֶם עוֹלָמוֹ וּמִכֻּלָּם עוֹשֶׂה סְגֻלָּה לְרַחֵם בִּשְׁבִילָם, וַהֲרֵי זוֹ הַמִּדָּה כּוֹלֶלֶת כָּל הַמִּדּוֹת כֻּלָּם כִּדְפֵרְשׁוּ בְּאִדְרָא. כָּךְ הָאָדָם יְתַקֵּן הַנְהָגָתוֹ עִם בְּנֵי אָדָם שֶׁאֲפִלּוּ שֶׁלֹּא יִמְצָא טַעֲנָה מֵאֵלּוּ הַנִּזְכָּרוֹת יֹאמַר כְּבָר הָיוּ שָׁעָה קֹדֶם שֶׁלֹּא חָטְאוּ וַהֲרֵי אוֹתָהּ הַשָּׁעָה אוֹ בְּיָמִים קַדְמוֹנִים הָיוּ כְּשֵׁרִים וְיִזְכֹּר לָהֶם הַטּוֹבָה שֶׁעָשׂוּ בְּקַטְנוּתָם וְיִזְכֹּר לָהֶם אַהֲבַת גְּמוּלֵי מֵחָלָב עַתִּיקֵי מִשָּׁדָיִם וּבָזֶה לֹא יִמָּצֵא אָדָם שֶׁאֵינוֹ רָאוּי לְהֵטִיבוֹ וּלְהִתְפַּלֵּל עַל שְׁלוֹמוֹ וּלְרַחֵם עָלָיו.

The Thirteenth Level

From Days of Old

Behold, this is a trait for God with the Jewish people: when they have exhausted the merit of their ancestors and the like, what does God do? Behold, on their own merit they are unworthy. It is written: *I remembered you, the kindness of your youth, the love when you were a bride.*

God literally remembers the early days, the love that once was, and shows mercy to the Jewish people. In this manner God recalls for their benefit all the commandments they performed from the day they were born, and all the positive Levels with which God causes the universe to function for them. Out of all this, God creates a special method to show them mercy, an Level that includes all of the previous Levels, as is explained in the *Idra*. So too should a person perfect one's dealings with other people. Even if one cannot find any reason from all of the preceding, one should say, "there was once a time when this person did not sin. At that moment, or in those early days, this person was good." One should think of the good things the other person did as a child, and recall the love that one has for the child who is yet nursing. With this method, one will not be able to find a person who is undeserving of benefit, unworthy of prayer and mercy.

Commentary

The Thirteen Levels conclude with a final, irrefutable argument for forgiveness, along with a strategy that addresses the most difficult cases. The Twelfth Level describes how God uses ancestral merit to generate forgiveness, but what if, God forbid, even that merit is exhausted? If there is no longer any supply of ancestral merit, God looks back on a time when the sinner was certainly innocent, either as a child or, if necessary, as a baby. Comparing himself to a husband, God remembers the strength of the love he had for his bride in the early days of the marriage, and uses those profound memories to find space for mercy. Like an aggrieved husband, he finds a way to tolerate his wife's current misbehavior by remembering how it was between them when they were first married.

The Thirteenth Level counsels us to do the same with difficult people. Even when a person really has no personal merit to speak of, and has gone so far as to even use up all ancestral merit, there is always the recourse of remembering that the person was, at one time, an innocent child. Who knows what cruelties were inflicted on this child to make them turn out so badly? Who knows what poor choices were made by the child that sent him or her into a spiral of decline? At some point in their lives, however, this person was wholly and immediately good.

Many years ago, I taught at the Middle School level in order to help make ends meet for my family. Teaching a class of 12-year olds was an exceptionally difficult assignment, far harder than any class I ever taught at the University level. One year I had a student who was particularly difficult—ill-behaved, disrespectful, and an instigator of a significant amount of classroom antics. He was a hard, obstinate, and even misanthropic child, and having him in the class was sheer torture.

One day I happened to be in the playground during recess, casually reading while the boys played basketball. I didn't see the play, but somehow a basket was scored or a shot was missed that favored one team. A ruckus of raised voices ensued, and I turned to see what was going on. To my shock and surprise, the tough kid was crying openly, weeping and even blubbering, like a child of seven or eight. He was perhaps as tall as I was, but his physique was far beyond his emotional maturity. It suddenly appeared to me that I caught a glimpse of his fragile soul, wounded over something as small as a basketball game. Seeing him as the child that he was, it was impossible to hold any anger or resentment in my heart for him.

Rabbi Shaynberg notes that the Thirteenth Level is the greatest of them all because it is so contrary to human nature. Nevertheless, at the same time it is the most powerful of the Levels, "a Level that includes all the Levels," because it is impossible to imagine a person that did not have a moment of total innocence, and thus merit forgiveness.

Practical Application

When all else fails: imagine him or her as a child, or a nursing baby. Can you really be angry with him?

Conclusion

עַד כַּאן הִגִּיעַ שְׁלֹשׁ עֶשְׂרֵה מִדּוֹת שֶׁבָּהֶן יִהְיֶה הָאָדָם דּוֹמֶה אֶל קוֹנוֹ שֶׁהֵן מִדּוֹת שֶׁל רַחֲמִים עֶלְיוֹנוֹת וּסְגֻלָּתָן כִּי כְּמוֹ שֶׁיִּהְיֶה הָאָדָם מִתְנַהֵג לְמַטָּה כָּךְ יִזְכֶּה לִפְתֹּחַ לוֹ מִדָּה עֶלְיוֹנָה מִלְמַעְלָה מַמָּשׁ כְּפִי מַה שֶּׁיִּתְנַהֵג כָּךְ מַשְׁפִּיעַ מִלְמַעְלָה וְגוֹרֵם שֶׁאוֹתָהּ הַמִּדָּה תָּאִיר בָּעוֹלָם. וּלְכָךְ אַל יָלוּזוּ מֵעֵינֵי הַשֵּׂכֶל שְׁלֹשׁ עֶשְׂרֵה מִדּוֹת אֵלּוּ וְהַפָּסוּק לֹא יָסוּף מִפִּיו כְּדֵי שֶׁיִּהְיֶה לוֹ לְמַזְכֶּרֶת כַּאֲשֶׁר יָבֹא לוֹ מַעֲשֶׂה שֶׁיִּצְטָרֵךְ לְהִשְׁתַּמֵּשׁ בְּמִדָּה אַחַת מֵהֶן יִזְכֹּר וְיֹאמַר הֲרֵי דָּבָר זֶה תָּלוּי בְּמִדָּה פְּלוֹנִית אֵינִי רוֹצֶה לָזוּז מִמֶּנָּה שֶׁלֹּא תִּתְעַלֵּם וְתִסְתַּלֵּק הַמִּדָּה הַהִיא מִן הָעוֹלָם:

Conclusion

Conclusion

This concludes the Thirteen Levels, by which a human may imitate the Creator, which are the Higher Traits of Mercy. Their precious value: if one behaves according to them in this world, this will open up the corresponding trait on high. Precisely as one behaves, one will cause the flow from above, and cause that trait to illuminate the world.

Therefore one should not lose consciousness of these Thirteen Levels, and the verse should not leave one's mouth, so that it will serve as a reminder. When one encounters a situation when one needs to employ one of the Levels, let one remember and say "behold, this matter requires the use of this Level, and I do not wish to move away from it, such that this Level not be hidden or removed from the Universe."

Commentary

Rabbi Cordovero clearly indicated that *Date Palm of Devorah* was not some theoretical treatise, useful only as a guide to higher kabbalistic principles. It is a practical work, intended for application in the real world, and its readers are urged to commit the Thirteen Levels to memory and recall them when confronted with the challenges of living in a social environment. Many commentators, therefore, have traditionally included a short summary of the Levels, with short descriptions of their meaning, and this work will follow in the tradition.

1. The Insulted King: *reflect on God's tolerance.*

2. Let it Go for Now: *give people a chance to fix things on their own.*

3. Take Care of it Personally: *do not delegate forgiveness.*

4. Remember the Family: *we are all connected.*

5. Release the Anger: *recognize that change is hard.*

6. Who Makes Your Lunch? *recognize every kindnesses.*

7. A Knot is Stronger: *when they return, love them more, not less.*

8. Maintain a Core of Love: *don't let offense live rent-free in your head.*

9. Bury the Past: *perform symbolic acts of forgiveness.*

10. Do the Right Thing Anyway: *that's the best they can do.*

11. Do More for Those who Do More: *recognize their sacrifice.*

12. Remember Where They Came From: *their ancestors were*

good.

13. The Moment of Innocence: *everyone was a child once.*

A Note on the Text

This edition of *Date Palm of Devorah* is based on the critical edition published by Betsalel Bezek and Noam Samet (Kulmos, 2002). *Date Palm of Devorah* was first published in 1588, almost twenty years after Rabbi Cordovero's passing. The *editio princeps* contains several errors, many of which were repeated in over seventy editions published since the 16th century. It is impossible to ascertain which of these errors stem from the original manuscript and which were the result of later editions.

Eleven handwritten manuscripts survive; unfortunately none of them in the author's own hand, but three of them date from the 16th century, and are invaluable in the determination of the most accurate text of *Date Palm of Devorah*. The present text reflects the painstaking effort of my student, Ms. Yiska Sandbrand, who carefully compared a modern edition with the first printing of *Tomer Devorah* and identified all of the variant readings. The text was further improved by a careful examination of the revised text with the Bezek and Samet edition, incorporating numerous changes suggested by the three surviving 16th-century manuscripts. The Hebrew text is vowelized for greater accessibility (the original does not have vowels, and the spelling there is generally written *plene*), but when emending the text I have indicated my changes by omitting vowels. Although there are many corrections, the distinctions are primarily grammatical in nature, and do not change the essential meaning of the text.

One of the more obvious discrepancies between the various printed editions of *Date Palm of Devorah* is the use of paragraph breaks. First issued in the early years of publishing, the *editio princeps* is printed in one solid block of text justified on both left and right, probably as a cost-saving measure. Paragraph breaks in this early printing are indicated by slashes (\), presumably adapted from the author's original manuscript, now lost. These paragraph breaks seem quite idiosyncratic, with frequent use of single-sentence paragraphs mixed with long, uninterrupted passages. The Hebrew text presented in *The Kabbalah of Forgiveness* preserves these paragraph breaks, but the English translation has been adapted to more contemporary and conventional usage.

I have taken some liberties with this translation. First, *The Kabbalah of Forgiveness* represents a treatment of the large initial chapter of *Date Palm of Devorah*, without continuing through the smaller chapters two through ten. The latter chapters are thematically related to *Date Palm of Devorah*, but they are far more complex and require much more scholarly support apparatus to be comprehended by readers less familiar with Cordoveran Kabbalah and rabbinic literature in general. Several other students of *Date Palm of Devorah* have also followed this approach, completely omitting discussion of the latter two-thirds of the original.

I have also maintained the traditional spelling of Rabbi Moshe Cordovero's name, although Dr. Zohar Raviv has conclusively demonstrated that the author and his son consistently signed their name in the Portuguese form Cordoeiro (קורדואירו). The Spanish spelling has been the commonly accepted version of his name for over four centuries, and therefore I have chosen to remain consistent with standard usage.

Finally, and by way of apology, I have been unable to avoid completely the use of gendered language in my translation. Rabbi Cordovero's writings are filled with third person singular pronouns, and it proved far too onerous to translate consistently "he" as "he or she," "one," or "a person." This effort does not represent a sacrifice of fidelity, as Hebrew generalizes in the masculine such that "he" may often legitimately replaced by "one," but the resulting text was so stilted that I eventually abandoned the attempt.

Select Bibliography

Selected Commentaries and Translations

Ashkenazi, Ze'ev Volf, *Sefer Tomer Devorah* Jerusalem, 5688 (1927/1928).

Bezek, Betsalel and Noam Samet, *Sefer Tomer Devorah: yatsa le-or la-rishonah be-Vintsia shm"t ve-atah yotsei le-or me-hadash al pi kitvei-yad u-defus rishon be-tosefet mekorot ve-he'arot* Jerusalem: Jerusalem: Kolmus, 2002.

Feldbrand, S. *Middos: Inspiration, Stories and Practical Advice Based on Tomer Devorah* Lakewood: Israel Book Shop, 2007.

García i Amat, Núria, *Moshe ben Ya'acob Cordovero: La Palmera de Débora* Mataró, Spain: Indigo, 1998.

Gavra, Yisrael, *Sefer Tomer Devorah im perush ha-bahir gevia ha-zahav* Jerusalem: n.p., n.d.

Goldberg, Aharon David, *Ve-halakhta be-derakhav*, commentary printed under title *Sefer Tomer Devorah* Wickliffe, OH: Ohel Desktop Publishing, 5766 (2005/2006). Fifth printing.

Epstein, Ben Tsion, *Sefer Tomer Devorah im bi'ur hakdamot u-she'arim* Jerusalem: n.p., 2013.

Jacobs, Louis, *The Palm Tree of Deborah, translated from the Hebrew with an introduction and notes* New York: Sepher-Hermon Press, 1981 (first published 1960).

Landau, Moshe David Yehezkel, *13 midot: Tomer Devorah Perek Rishon* B'nei Brak: n.p., 2004.

Miller, Moshe, *Date Palm of Devorah* Jerusalem: Targum/ Feldheim, 1993.

Mopsik, Charles, *Le Palmier de Déborah* Paris: Verdier, 1985.

Schäfer, Klaus, *Rabbi Moses Cordovero von Zefat: Tomer Devorah—Der Palmbaum der Deborah*, German translation by Klaus Schäfer and Shulamit Zemach-Tendler, Freiburg im Breisgau: Lambertus, 2003.

Shaynberg, Mordechai, *Sefer Tomer Devorah im pirush vayomer moshe* [Jerusalem?]: Da'at, 2003.

Solomon, Matityahu Hayim, *Matnat hayim*, commentary printed under title *Sefer Tomer Devorah* Wickliffe, OH: Ohel Desktop Publishing, 5766 (2005/2006). Fifth printing.

Waxman, Nissan, *Sefer Tomer Devorah* New York: Shoshanim, 1960.

Yudaikin, Shmuel Yitshak Gad ha-Kohen, *Sefer Tomer Devorah im perush shomer ha-pardes/Shivhei ha-Remak* B'nei Brak: Da'at Kedoshim, 5763 (2002/2003).

Related Works

Ben-Shlomo, Yosef, *Torat ha-elohut shel R' Moshe Kordovero* Jerusalem: Mosad Bialik, 1965.

Cordovero, Moshe, *Sefer Eilima Rabati* Jerusalem: Yisrael Levi Alboim, 1966.

Dan, Joseph, "'No Evil Descends from Heaven:' Sixteenth-Century Jewish Concepts of Evil," in Bernard Dov

Cooperman, ed., *Jewish Thought in the Sixteenth Century* Cambridge, MA: Harvard University Press, 1983, 89-104.

Dan, Joseph, *Jewish Mysticism and Jewish Ethics*, Seattle: University of Washington Press, 1985.

Fine, Lawrence, ed., *Safed Spirituality: Rules of Mystical Piety, The Beginning of Wisdom* New York: Paulist Press, 1984.

Horodetsky, S. A., *Torat ha-Kabalah shel Rabi Moshe Kordovero* Berlin: Eshkol, 1924.

Raviv, Zohar, *Decoding the Dogma Within the Enigma: The Life, Works, Mystical Piety and Systematic Thought of Rabbi Moses Cordoeiro (aka Cordovero; Safed, Israel, 1522-1570)* Berlin: VDM Verlag Dr. Müller, 2008.

Robinson, Ira, *Moshe Cordovero's Introduction to Kabbalah: An Annotated Translation of his* Or Ne'erav New York: Yeshiva University Press, 1994.

Sack, Bracha, *Be'sha'arei ha-kabalah shel Rabi Moshe Kordovero* Jerusalem: Bialik, 1995.

Sack, Bracha, "The Influence of Cordovero on Seventeenth-Century Jewish Thought," in Bernard Dov Cooperman, ed., *Jewish Thought in the Seventeenth Century*, Cambridge MA: Harvard University Press, 365-380.

Werblowsky, R. J. Zwi, "The Safed Revival and Its Aftermath," in *Jewish Spirituality* Volume Two: From the Sixteenth-Century Revival to the Present, New York: Crossroad, 1989, 7-33.

Acknowledgements

My gratitude to the Source of all Blessing, who has given me life, and preserved me, and allowed me to reach this moment.

The flaws in this book are mine alone, but its merits are the result of extensive collaboration with teachers, colleagues, and students. First and foremost I must thank my beloved wife Ilana Tirzah and our children Raphaela Meirit, Danit Malka, Aliza Shoshana, Alexander Eliyahu, Boaz Uziel and Aryeh Yitzhak. The everyday challenges of life in a large family are a living laboratory for forgiveness, and I am especially grateful to my daughters who contributed written comments on several versions of the manuscript. Rabbi Moshe Gruenstein of Young Israel and Rabbi Sholom Dovber Lipskar of The Shul graciously read early versions and provided useful suggestions. Dr. Yaakov (Koby) Frances, Dr. Stefanie Herron, and Dr. Lee Williams, my colleagues in the Touro College South Writer's Group, spent hours refining the text to make it both comprehensible in content and graceful in from. I have been fortunate to have led several study sessions in this text, most notably an all-night Shavuot marathon at the Young Israel, and I thank my dedicated adult students David Herman, Bev Kagan, Susan Leaventon, Ruthy Marks, Betsalel Ness, Penny Pasch, Marc Sternbaum, Myriam Wiener, and Eileen Yasbin. Freda Greenbaum and Rachel Herman read portions of the MS and offered encouragement, as did my close friends Isaac Arber and Aryeh Wuensch. Finally, I have enjoyed the privilege of introducing Rabbi Cordovero's thought to several undergraduates at Touro College South over the years: Naomi Abergel, Sivan Azran, Chaya Brody, Yeshayahu Gruberger, Ahuva Katzin, Vanessa Khoudari, Aharon Laks,

Daneal Lugerner, Michael Neuman, Malkie Nodel, Chana Russo-Fabian, Sheina Schochet, Rachel Shakibpanah, and BB Yachnes. Special thanks must go to several advanced students, including my daughter Danit Malka (an extremely dedicated student of *Date Palm of Devorah*), Perel Gross, Shiran Malul, Amit Subar, Gerardo Rodriguez, and Zohar Peleg. Yiska Sandbrand painstakingly compared the 1588 *editio princeps* with the current vocalized edition, a difficult task that improved the fidelity of the text used in this translation. On many occasions their critiques successfully challenged my assumptions, and their enthusiasm for *The Kabbalah of Forgiveness* continues to inspire me.

HMA
Surfside, FL
Adar I 5774/February 2014

Acknowledgements for the Second Edition

I am grateful to Ms. Jésica Neuah and Rabbi Abraham Serruyah of Editorial Perspectivas for suggesting a Spanish translation of this work, so beautifully written by Ms. Sara Efrati. Ms. Rebecca Odessa, created haunting and inspiring interpretations of the Thirteen Levels that allowed me to view the work of Rabbi Cordovero with an entirely different perspective: her art graces this new cover. Rabbi Ya'akov Trump of the Young Israel of Lawrence-Cedarhurst served as a Rabbinic sounding board, bringing to our discussions of *Date Palm of Devorah* a wealth of knowledge from both traditional Jewish sources and current research in Positive Psychology. Thanks must also go to two new members of the family: Chaim Yaakov Singer, my son-in-law and study partner in Maimonides; and Binyamin Mills, my son-in-law and study partner in Rabbi Cordovero.

Photo: Marko Dashev

Henry Abramson earned his PhD at the University of Toronto in 1995 with a dissertation on the Jews of Ukraine, later published jointly by the Harvard Ukrainian Research Institute and the Center for Jewish Studies at Harvard University and in Ukrainian translation by Dukh i Litera. He studied at Yeshivat Ohr Somayach in Toronto, Jerusalem and Monsey, NY, and has held visiting appointments and doctoral fellowships at Cornell, Harvard, Oxford and the Hebrew University of Jerusalem. His research has been supported by fellowships from the Social Sciences and Research Council of Canada, the National Endowment for the Humanities, the United States Holocaust Memorial Museum, and he received the Excellence in the Academy Award from the National Education Association. He currently serves as Dean at the mighty Avenue J campus of Touro's Lander College of Arts and Sciences in Brooklyn, New York.

Made in the USA
Monee, IL
08 September 2022